The Glory and Power of His Presence

Bruce D. Reekie

Sovereign World

Sovereign World Ltd
PO Box 777
Tonbridge
Kent TN11 9XT
England

ISBN: 1 85240 169 9

Typeset by CRB Associates, Norwich
Printed in England by Clays Ltd, St Ives plc

Contents

If you enjoy this book and would like to help us to send a
copy of it and many other titles to needy pastors in the
Third World, please write for further information
or send your gift to:

Sovereign World Trust
PO Box 777, Tonbridge
Kent TN11 9XT
United Kingdom

or to the **'Sovereign World'** distributor in your country.

If sending money from outside the United Kingdom,
please send an International Money Order or Foreign
Bank Draft in STERLING, drawn on a **UK** bank to
Sovereign World Trust.

Foreword

There is no question that something remarkable is happening in the church at the end of the twentieth century. It is more than growth in the numbers and size of congregations. It is more than increasing influence in communities or the rise of effective ministries. While the church is probably bigger, brighter and better than it has been there is something more significant taking place.

The manifest presence of God is occurring whenever and wherever His people gather, and it is happening more frequently and powerfully than most of this generation have ever seen.

Most revivalist movements began in the incandescent glory of the Lord. His overwhelming presence attended by astonishing manifestations of divine power arrested the attention of people and aroused their hunger for a more fulfilling relationship with Him. They moved out of cold and clinical religion to form new fellowships dedicated to the presence of God. They discovered that one moment of God's glory would re-orient a seeking heart more than most of the procedures and practices of routine religion could in a life-time.

Unfortunately many of these 'revival people' gradually moved away from the manifest presence of God to something less demanding, and easier to schedule. Their church life once again assumed a more predictable pose, but became sanitised, sterile and safe. The 'presence of God' in the midst became little more than the nice feeling generated by a group with similar values.

But God's manifest presence, His awesome glory is rising throughout the church world-wide, and it isn't safe, sombre and static. His presence has become strong and conspicuous. The manifestations of His power cannot be ignored. He has overwhelmed the programs of thousands of churches and breathed new life into 'dead bones'. They are rising up like a mighty army, infused with reality instead of remote religion and the world is feeling the impact of God's people who have tasted the glory of the Lord.

I have personally experienced this mighty visitation from heaven and declare without doubt that God is among His people in a fresh, new way. The demonstration of this glory separates one from past satisfactions and draws us out in anticipation of what is yet to come.

John Wesley declared that 'the best is yet to be' and I heartily agree. The Holy Spirit has come to us again to lead us from glory to glory. His intention for the church is for it to become a reflection of His glory and manifest His presence to the world.

Bruce Reekie has addressed this issue powerfully. This book says it all – without the glory of God openly manifest, the church becomes an aberration, or something else than what it was intended to be. Bruce has demonstrated a commitment to the presence of God over a long time and refuses to capitulate to the corroding influences of a religious exercise. He has shown a consistent hunger for the God of Glory since his youth.

I commend this book to all who seek for more.

Dr David Cartledge
Chairman of the
Australian Pentecostal Ministers' Fellowship
President of Southern Cross Bible College

Chapter 1

The Earth Shall Be Filled

'In the beginning God created the heavens and the earth.' The very first verse of the Bible distinguishes the earth from the rest of the heavens, thereby highlighting the unique place the earth holds in the eternal purpose of God.

Out of the whole universe of stars, galaxies and solar systems, the Lord chose one planet – earth – as a home for His man and a theatre for His Glory. Life on planet earth was designed to be an extension of life in Heaven. For example, the language of Genesis 2:8; *'The Lord God planted a Garden eastward in Eden,'* suggests a transplantation of Heaven's flora.

The Bible abounds with references to the special relationship or Divine connection between **Heaven** and **Earth**. One such example is found in our Lord's sermon on the mount:

> *'But I say to you, do not swear at all: neither by heaven, for it is God's throne; nor by earth, for it is His footstool; nor by Jerusalem, for it is the city of the great King.'*   (Matthew 5:34, 35)

The 'third heaven' or the 'Heaven of heavens' is God's throne; the command and control centre of the universe. The earth is God's footstool; a colony of Heaven. Jerusalem is the city of the great King; the earthly capital of the Kingdom of God.

The original prescription for creation was 'Heaven on earth'. Life on earth was intended to be a reflection of the glorious life of Heaven. Thus, the disciples' prayer of Matthew chapter six, takes on restorative dimensions: *'Your Kingdom come, Your will be done on Earth as it is in Heaven.'* Life, according to the quality of its original design: an extension of the righteousness, peace and joy of Heaven.

In His Image

The first man, Adam, was created in the image and according to the likeness of God. The process of creation is described in Genesis 2:7;

> *'And the LORD God formed man of the dust of the ground, and breathed into his nostrils the breath of life; and man became a living being.'*

First the natural, then the spiritual. God formed Adam's body from the dust of the earth, and then breathed into that empty shell the 'breath of life'. The phrase, 'breath of life' (Hebrew *'ruwach'*), denotes God's own spirit-nature, elsewhere referred to as 'eternal life'.

Adam was created in righteousness and holiness; a child of God and a partaker of the Divine Nature, with the seed of eternal life in his heart. As a result, the creature walked in perfect fellowship with the Creator. Spirit communed with spirit.

The original union of God and man is best depicted by the New Testament analogy of the vine and the branches (John 15). Vitally joined in eternal life; one spirit with the Lord; receiving of His fullness; partaking of His righteous nature; sharing in His holy character; maturing in the image of God.

According to Scripture, Adam and Eve were naked, and were not ashamed. However, the nakedness of which the

Bible speaks, that of primeval innocence, had a peculiar quality unknown to modern, fallen man.

Adam and Eve had no need of clothing, because they were clothed with the Glory of God. Psalm 104:1, 2 declares:

> '... O LORD my God, You are very great. You are clothed with honour and majesty, Who cover Yourself with light as with a garment...'

Because Adam and Eve were created in the image of God, they shared His clothing of honour and majesty, and His covering of light. In the ensuing pages of Scripture, we catch rare glimpses of the original covering of Glory.

On one such occasion, Moses spent forty days and nights on Mount Sinai, during which time the Lord descended in a cloud and caused His Glory to pass by in a wonderful revelation of His nature and power.

Unbeknown to Moses, when he came down from the mountain with the two Tablets of the Testimony in his hand, the skin of his face shone with the reflection of the Glory of God! So much so, that the children of Israel were afraid to come near Moses, thus prompting him to cover his face with a veil! (Exodus 34).

The most notable example of a covering of Glory is found in the life of the Lord Jesus, in the incident of the 'Transfiguration on the Mount'.

> 'Now after six days Jesus took Peter, James, and John his brother, led them up on a high mountain by themselves; and he was transfigured before them. His face shone like the sun, and His clothes became as white as the light.'   (Matthew 17:1, 2)

The Greek word *'metamorphoo'*, translated 'transfigure', means to 'change into another form'. The eminent Greek scholar, Kenneth Wuest, makes the following comments in volume one of *Word Studies in the Greek New Testament*:

'... The simple verb refers to the act of giving outward expression of one's inner character, that outward expression coming from and being truly representative of that inner character .... The translation expanded, thus reads, *"The manner of His outward expression was changed before them, that outward expression coming from and being truly representative of His inner nature."*

... Out from within the inmost being of the Son of God, there shone that dazzling glory of the essence of Deity which He possesses co-eternally with God the Father and God the Spirit. It shone right through the clay walls of His humanity and through the clothing He wore .... This effulgence of glory came from within, and was an inherent possession of the Lord of Glory ... this is what is meant by the transfiguration of the Lord Jesus.'[1]

The effulgence of the Divine Nature covered Jesus' physical person like a garment. Such was the glory that clothed Adam and Eve in the Garden of Eden!

Be Fruitful and Multiply

The rudimental command to *'Be fruitful and multiply, fill the earth and subdue it, and have dominion'* (Genesis 1:28), was given to man in his perfect state, and should be interpreted accordingly.

As partakers of the Divine Nature, Adam and Eve were commissioned to reproduce after their kind – children, born in the image of God, having the Divine Seed in their hearts.

Beginning in Eden, the holy family was to 'be fruitful and multiply', the phrase connoting reproduction and dissemination. Moreover, as they spread abroad over the face of the earth they were to 'subdue and have dominion', terms that bespeak conquest and rulership.

Adam was God's vice-regent, and on his shoulders rested the responsibility of establishing and administering the

Kingdom of Heaven on planet earth. Herein lies the essence of the Genesis 1:28 ordinance.

Adam's children were intended to be ambassadors of the Kingdom. Whithersoever they went, they were to introduce Kingdom Life, administer Kingdom Law, and establish Kingdom Order. They were to be carriers of the Presence and Glory of God; conveyors of His Nature and Power.

Through the outreach and witness of these God-like ones, the earth would be filled with the Glory of the Lord – the revelation of the attributes of the Creator. The earth would become one great amphitheatre of praise and worship. Joy and peace and righteousness would flow like a river among the nations.

'As in Heaven, so on earth'. Through the propagation and ministry of the holy family, earth would realize its destiny as a colony of Heaven. Such was the dream of God for His people. Yet, due to the intrusion of Satan and the contamination of sin, it was not to be.

Man's disobedience to God's Word and rebellion against God's authority not only cost him his place in the Garden of Eden, but more importantly, his place in the Kingdom of Heaven.

The expulsion from Paradise was an outward sign of an inner reality: *'In the day that you eat of it you shall surely die'* (Genesis 2:17). Spiritual death. Eternal separation from God.

The Apostle Paul uses the following phrases to describe the gravity of man's fallen state:

> *'And you ... were dead in trespasses and sins, in which you once walked according to the course of this world, according to the prince of the power of the air, the spirit who now works in the sons of disobedience, among whom we all once conducted ourselves in the lusts of the flesh, fulfilling the desires of the flesh and of the mind, and were by nature children of wrath ... '*

(Ephesians 2:1–3)

Cut off from the Presence of God; subject to the dominion of darkness; having a nature with a propensity toward rebellion and sin; therefore, an enemy of God and an object of His wrath!

Paul elaborates on man's hopeless condition in Ephesians 4:17–19;

> '... *the Gentiles walk, in the futility of their mind, having their understanding darkened, being alienated from the life of God, because of the ignorance that is in them, because of the blindness of their heart; who, being past feeling, have given themselves over to lewdness, to work all uncleanness with greediness.*'

Minds that are in a state of war with the Almighty, being filled with foolish notions and godless philosophies; powers of discernment clouded with darkness, being as it were, spiritually blindfolded. Having no share in the Spirit-nature of God, which is Eternal Life; hearts that are hardened and consciences that are seared, thus rendering one insensible to moral conviction; totally abandoned to sensuality, thus leading to excessive practices of all sorts of immorality.

> '*In the world without hope and without God!*'
>
> (Ephesians 2:12)

As Truly As I Live

Despite man's abject failure, God never abandoned His dream of having a people among whom He could dwell and through whom He could reveal His Glory.

In the final analysis, the fulfilment of God's purpose is dependent on God Himself, not man. It is '*not by human might or power, but by the Spirit of the Lord*' (Zechariah 4:6). God must, of course, find a man who will co-operate with Him and perform His will, but it is '*the zeal of the Lord of hosts that will bring it to pass*' (Isaiah 37:32).

The phrase, *'the zeal of the Lord'*, denotes the tenacity of God's Holy Spirit in the face of satanic opposition. Despite setbacks and reversals, God has never deviated from His selected course. With unswerving determination, He pursues His desired objective.

The Lord God, Himself, stands as the surety of His Word:

> *'By Myself I have sworn, says the* LORD *... blessing I will bless you, and multiplying I will multiply your descendants as the stars of the heaven and as the sand which is on the seashore; and your descendants shall possess the gates of their enemies. In your seed all the nations of the earth shall be blessed...'*
>
> (Genesis 22:16–18)

Notice that God says, *'By Myself I have sworn,'* and then annunciates the course of world redemption: covenant relationship with a man named Abraham, from whom will issue a nation, Israel, out of whose midst will arise the Messiah, Jesus, who will be God's blessing of salvation unto the ends of the earth.

Referring to this promise, the writer to the Hebrews says that God swore by Himself, because He could swear by no one greater (Hebrews 6:13).

> *'But truly, as I live, all the earth shall be filled with the glory of the* LORD.*'*   (Numbers 14:21)

One could be excused for assuming that God would make such a declaration when Israel's faith and obedience was at its peak. However, precisely the opposite was the case.

Israel had just failed God miserably through unbelief and disobedience, thus prompting God to pass a suspended sentence of death on almost an entire generation! Yet, in the midst of a disaster of satanic deception and human ineptitude, the Lord recommits Himself to His eternal purpose.

Notice that God does not say, 'But as truly as you live.' If it depended on man, it would never happen! Rather, *'But truly as I live, says the LORD.'* Once again, God swears by Himself.

The whole of God's enterprise is contingent on His faithfulness, His power, His wisdom and His ability! And in His faithfulness, God will raise up a people to co-operate with Him in His Kingdom purpose.

> *'The glory of the LORD shall be revealed, and all flesh shall see it together; for the mouth of the LORD has spoken.'*   (Isaiah 40:5)

'The glory of the LORD shall be revealed and all flesh shall see it together!' A wonderful promise, but what is the guarantee of its fulfilment? *'The mouth of the LORD has spoken!'* The fact that Almighty God is the One who said it. And the One who said it, watches over His Word to bring it to pass. (Jeremiah 1:12).

Restoration Strategy

Before the dust of death had a chance to settle, God stepped into the fall-out of Adam's transgression in the Garden to activate His rescue plan. This 'restoration strategy', conceived in the eternal council of the Triune God, called for a scapegoat and a sin offering; a substitutionary sacrifice that was blameless and undefiled.

In the first instance, innocent animals were sacrificed to provide garments of skin as a covering for Adam and Eve. From the erstwhile paradise, now invaded and devastated by sin, flowed a bloody trail of covenantal atonement, culminating some four thousand years later, on a lonely hill outside Jerusalem.

There, on the mountains of Moriah, God fulfilled His ancient covenant with Abraham. There, the spotless Son of God was offered as a Lamb for the sins of the world. What the blood of bulls and goats and other sacrificial animals could only foreshadow, the Blood of Messiah accomplished; namely, the remission of sin and the procurement of redemption. In the words of Paul, Messiah Jesus was *'delivered up because of our offences, and was raised because of our justification'* (Romans 4:25).

Moses' tabernacle in the wilderness, David's tabernacle on Mount Zion, and Solomon's temple on Mount Moriah, were stations on the way to the realization of God's dream of having a people among whom He could dwell and through whom He could reveal His Glory.

But it was not until *Shavuot* (the Day of Pentecost), AD 32, when the Holy Spirit was poured out on 120 disciples in an upper room in Jerusalem, that God's purpose came to fruition.

Finally, and for the first time in history, God had a body of men and women who were made in His image, according to His likeness. Finally, the dwelling place of God was with men – not in buildings of wood and stone, but in a spiritual temple of living stones – people who were redeemed by the Blood of the Lamb and recreated by the power of the Spirit.

Finally, God had a house in which to dwell that was not limited to time and space. *'You will not worship the Father in Jerusalem according to the old order; rather, all over the world people will worship the Father in spirit and in truth'* (John 4:21, 23 paraphrased).

The commission of Jesus to His disciples in Matthew 28:18–20 and Mark 16:15, is the New Testament counterpart to and the spiritual fulfilment of the original commission of God to Adam and Eve in Genesis 1:28.

Observe the correspondence between the two passages: *'Be fruitful, multiply, fill the earth* – Go into all the world ... all nations ... to every creature'; *'Subdue it, have dominion* – Preach the Gospel ... make disciples'.

The Gospel that we are to proclaim is the 'Gospel of the Kingdom'. It is the proclamation of the reign of God (Isaiah 52:7). Moreover, disciples are 'Kingdom subjects' – people who are disciplined to walk in the ways of the Lord. Jesus was saying to His followers:

'All authority has been given to Me; I am Lord and King. I appoint you as My ambassadors; the delegates of My authority and power in the earth. Go into all the world and proclaim My Lordship; administer My Kingdom; execute My dominion. Wherever you go, take My Presence and reveal My Glory.'

To these new creatures in Messiah, freshly created in God's image in righteousness and holiness, partakers of the Divine Nature of eternal life, filled with the Spirit (breath) of the Almighty, was given the privilege of fulfilling God's eternal purpose. And it is a privilege that is extended to all disciples of all generations.

As the Waters Cover the Sea

I asked the Lord, on one occasion, to explain the difference between the first outpouring of the Spirit at Pentecost, and the last outpouring of the Spirit before the return of the Lord Jesus.

The Lord showed me that the first outpouring of the Spirit was **localized** – in one place (Jerusalem), at one time (Pentecost), upon one ethnic group (Jews) – whereas, the last outpouring of the Spirit will be **universal** – upon all people groups and all nations, at the same time.

The Holy Spirit will be poured out on all flesh, **simultaneously**, in ultimate fulfilment of Joel's prophecy (Joel 2:28, 29). Every city, town and village will have its own unique 'Jerusalem Pentecost'. For the first time in history, there will be a truly **world-wide** movement of God's Spirit.

Every community will experience a witness of the Gospel and a manifestation of the Glory of God. According to the words of Jesus in Matthew 24:14, this is the scenario that will precipitate His second coming and the end of the age.

In the vision of the Revelation, the Apostle John saw a great multitude which no one could number – redeemed representatives from every nation, tribe, people and tongue

– standing before the Throne of God and the Lamb (Revelation 7:9).

Jesus said to go into *all the world*, and preach the Gospel to *every creature*, and make disciples of *all nations* (Greek: *'ethnos'*, people group). At the time of writing, there are an estimated 3,915 'unreached' people groups in the world – groups distinguishable by race, language, geography or culture that are unevangelized (with no definite witness of the Gospel) or unreached (with no significant response to the Gospel).[2]

Quite obviously, the spiritual outpouring of which Joel speaks, and the international ingathering of which John writes, has in its fullest sense, yet to take place.

> *'For the earth will be filled with the knowledge of the glory of the LORD, as the waters cover the sea.'*
> (Habakkuk 2:14)

A key-word breakdown of this verse yields a treasure chest of revelation! The Hebrew word *'male'*, translated 'filled', means to 'fill up to the brim', or 'thoroughly saturate'. *'Yada'*, the Hebrew word translated 'knowledge', denotes 'knowledge that is gained through close observation or firsthand experience', and often bespeaks 'intimate acquaintance'.

The Hebrew word *'kabod'*, translated 'glory', literally means 'weight' or 'heaviness'. Figuratively, it denotes 'the substance of God's Being'. Dr M.R. Vincent refers to the 'glory' as 'the expression of the Divine attributes collectively and the unfolded fullness of the Divine perfections.'

'Kabod' bespeaks 'the nature of God which is love, the character of God which is holiness, and the sovereignty of God which is power'.

Putting it all together, the Lord declares that the earth will be filled to overflowing or saturated with an intimate knowledge of the Glory of the Lord, through close observation and firsthand experience of the attributes and perfections of God's Being – the weight of His Personal Presence!

God likens the manifestation of His Glory to the waters of the sea: a voluminous tide that is beyond man's ability to control or measure.

From Glory to Glory

The New Testament indicates that the second coming of Messiah will not be a Divine rescue mission to snatch a struggling church out of the jaws of the Antichrist. The actual, physical return of our Lord and Saviour will be the consummation of God's program of revelation: the progressive manifestation of His Glory in the earth through Messiah's Body, the Church.

In the words of the Apostle Paul, Messiah is coming, in that day, *'to be glorified in His saints and to be admired among all those who believe'* (2 Thessalonians 1:10). The Second Coming is portrayed as a 'consummation of glory and power'; the completion of God's work of restoration throughout all ages and generations.

The concept of cumulative glory is espoused by the Apostle Paul in 2 Corinthians, chapter 3:

> *'But we all, with unveiled face, beholding as in a mirror the glory of the Lord, are being transformed into the same image from glory to glory, just as by the Spirit of the Lord.'*

The Amplified Bible puts it this way: *'... are constantly being transfigured into His very own image in ever increasing splendour and from one degree of glory to another ...'*

Our God is a God of growth and increase. 'From glory to glory' signifies God's plan of restoration for His people, and His desire to lead them, individually and corporately, into an ever increasing revelation of His nature and character, the end whereof is described in Ephesians 4:13–15 and Romans 8:29;

> *'...until we all attain oneness in the faith and in the experiential, full and precise knowledge of the Son of God, and reach mature manhood – the completeness of personality which is nothing less than the standard height of Christ's own perfection ... and grow up in every way and in all things into Him...'*

> *'For whom He foreknew, He also predestined to be moulded into the image of His Son and to share inwardly His likeness, that He might be the firstborn among many brethren.'*

The history of the Church since the time of the Reformation (16th Century) can best be understood in this light: a progressive restoration of Truth and an escalating revelation of the Glory of God.

According to this thesis, the generation of God's people who are alive at the time of Messiah's return will know the Lord more intimately, obey the Lord more fully, reflect the Lord's Glory more clearly, and administer the Lord's authority more faithfully than any preceding generation.

Powers of a Coming Age

The Bible describes the Holy Spirit of Promise as *'the guarantee of our inheritance until the redemption of the purchased possession'* (Ephesians 1:14). The Greek word *'arrabon'*, translated 'guarantee', is a business term that denotes earnest money, a down payment, a first instalment, a pledge, and a deposit.

In Romans 8:23, the Holy Spirit is spoken of as 'the firstfruits of the coming harvest,' or, in the words of Dr Moffatt, *'a foretaste of the future.'*

The writer to the Hebrews elaborates on this theme in chapter 6 and verses 4 through 5:

> *'...those who were once enlightened, and have tasted the heavenly gift, and have become partakers of the Holy*

> *Spirit, and have tasted the good word of God and the powers of the age to come ...'*

'Powers' is variously translated, 'mighty works', 'spiritual energies', 'strong influences', and 'spiritual resources' of the age to come. Thus, the gift of salvation, the power of the Holy Spirit, and the proclamation of God's Word is portrayed as **the Presence of the Future**; a foretaste and first instalment of ultimate Glory!

'The earth shall be filled with the Glory of the Lord.' The ultimate fulfilment of God's promise is bound up with and contingent upon the return of the Lord Jesus from Heaven. *'When Christ who is our life appears, **then** you will appear with Him in glory'* (Colossians 3:4).

However, God's call to Glory is **now**. Now we are children of God, though our true identity and destiny is yet to be fully revealed (1 John 3:2).

Now we are a house of God on earth, and His Presence is inhabiting our praises. Now God's Glory is arising upon His worshipping saints, and multitudes are coming to the light of salvation. Now the Gospel is being proclaimed throughout the world, demons are being expelled, and darkness scattered. Now righteousness and praise is springing forth in the sight of the nations.

'It does not yet appear what we shall be,' and 'we do not yet see all things put under His feet.' However, we can and should expect, in the final days of the outpouring of the Holy Spirit of Promise, a down payment of Glory that will shake the nations and fill the earth with a manifest Presence of Almighty God!

References

1. *Word Studies in the Greek New Testament* by Kenneth S. Wuest, Eerdmans Publishing Co., Volume 1, pp. 174–175.
2. *Operation World* by Patrick Johnstone, OM Publishing, fifth edition, p. 22.

Chapter 2

Jesus in the Midst

One day, as Jesus entered the region of Caesarea Philippi, an area renowned for its idolatry, having been dedicated by the Greeks to the mythological god Pan and by the Romans to the Emperor Augustus, He asked His disciples, *'Who do you say that I am?'*

Prompted by Divine revelation, Simon Peter answered, *'You are Messiah, the Son of the Living God!'* And upon this rock of revelation, Jesus staked His claim and pronounced His purpose:

> *'. . . on this rock I will build My church, and the gates of Hades shall not prevail against it.'*   (Matthew 16:18)

'I will build My church.' This little phrase represents the focus of human history; man's *raison d'être*. 'My church', as distinct from every other church. Therefore, it behoves us to discover the kind of church that Jesus is building.

'Ekklesia', the Greek word translated 'church', is 'an assembly of called out ones'. It was used among the Greeks to denote a body of citizens gathered together to discuss the affairs of state, and in Acts 19:32, of a riotous mob. Thus, *'ekklesia'* is a broad-based term that embraces any group of people gathered together in a commonality of purpose and action.

However, the distinguished nature of Jesus' church is delineated in Matthew 18:20;

> *'For where two or three are gathered together in My Name, I am there in the midst of them.'*

The chief characteristics of Jesus' church, as set forth in this passage, are His Lordship (*gathered together in My Name*) and His Presence (*I am there in the midst*).

The Name of Jesus is representative of His exalted glory and authority (Philippians 2:9–11 and Matthew 28:18–20). Therefore, to gather together in Jesus' Name is to assemble under His Lordship – representing all that He is and has! And to those who assemble under Jesus' Lordship, there is the promise of His manifest Presence in their midst.

The church that Jesus builds is a body of people bearing the distinctive marks of His government and His glory.

Among the Lampstands

'Jesus in the midst' is a favourite theme of New Testament writers, and in particular, of the beloved disciple John.

> *'Then, the same day at evening, being the first day of the week, when the doors were shut where the disciples were assembled, for fear of the Jews, Jesus came and stood in the midst, and said to them, "Peace be with you." When He had said this, He showed them His hands and His side. Then the disciples were glad when they saw the Lord. So Jesus said to them again, "Peace to you! As the Father has sent Me, I also send you." And when He had said this, He breathed on them, and said to them, "Receive the Holy Spirit. If you forgive the sins of any, they are forgiven them; if you retain the sins of any, they are retained."'* (John 20:19–23)

As in the beginning, when God breathed into Adam His own Spirit-nature of eternal life, so Jesus breathed upon and into the disciples *Ruwach HaKodesh* – the Spirit of the Life of God.

'Jesus in the midst' transformed a group of fearful, cowering disciples into a powerful apostolic company that was destined to proclaim the Gospel throughout the length and breadth of the known world and change the course of history.

The manifest Presence of Jesus ministered peace to the disciples – *Shalom* – spiritual strength, mental wholeness, emotional stability and physical health. Moreover, the manifest Presence of Jesus brought a fresh revelation of His aliveness, and hence, His Lordship over sin, death and hell, which, in turn, issued in a new mandate of Kingdom administration.

> *'And after eight days His disciples were again inside, and Thomas with them. Jesus came, the doors being shut, and stood in the midst, and said, "Peace to you!" Then He said to Thomas, "Reach your finger here, and look at My hands; and reach your hand here, and put it into My side. Do not be unbelieving, but believing." And Thomas answered and said to Him, "My Lord and my God!"'*
>
> (John 20:26–28)

From this story we learn that there is no door big enough to shut out the Presence of Him who is the Resurrection and the Life! Furthermore, the manifest Presence of Jesus is the catalyst of faith and obedience. A revelation of 'Jesus in the midst' banishes fear and doubt in favour of an abundance of Holy Spirit inspired hope and joy.

Many years later, as an old man in exile on the Isle of Patmos, John had a vision of the glorified Messiah:

> *'I was in the Spirit on the Lord's Day, and I heard behind me a loud voice, as of a trumpet, saying, "I am the Alpha and the Omega, the First and the Last..." Then I turned to see the voice that spoke with me. And having turned I saw seven golden lampstands, and in the*

midst of the seven lampstands One like the Son of Man...' (Revelation 1:10–13)

Once again, John sees Jesus in the midst of His people – this time, however, it is not a ragged group of harried disciples, cloistered in an upper room in Jerusalem, but the seven major churches of the Roman Province of Asia, representing all churches of all generations, that is, **The Church Universal**. Jesus stands in the midst as Head of the Church – the source of life and power; the focus of worship and service; the consummation of creation and redemption.

One of the hallmarks of a true movement of God's Spirit is the restoration of 'Jesus-centredness'. When Jesus is truly in the midst, everything revolves around and relates to Him. Conversely, an absence of the Presence of God spawns a man-centred (humanistic) Gospel and order of service. Hence, the current emphasis on 'self-esteem' in certain sections of the Church where human organization has replaced spiritual manifestation.

A revelation of 'Jesus in the midst' invariably releases a spirit of repentance, godly fear, humility and sacrificial obedience in the life of the congregation, as evidenced by the Apostle John, who, when he saw the Lord in the midst of the churches, fell at His feet as though he were dead.

Moreover, the Jesus who stands in the midst of the churches is not the meek and lowly carpenter of Nazareth, but the exalted Jesus of the Throne of God, crowned with glory and honour as King of kings and Lord of lords. Even John, who knew Him better and loved Him more than any other disciple, was astonished and overwhelmed by the Glory of His Presence.

'... One like the Son of Man, clothed with a garment down to the feet and girded about the chest with a golden band. His head and hair were white like wool, as white as snow, and His eyes were like a flame of fire; His feet were like fine brass, as if refined in a furnace, and His

voice as the sound of many waters. He had in His right hand seven stars, out of His mouth went a sharp two-edged sword, and His countenance was like the sun shining in its strength. And when I saw Him, I fell at His feet as dead. But He laid His right hand on me, saying to me, "Do not be afraid; I am the First and the Last. I am He who lives, and was dead, and behold, I am alive forevermore. Amen. And I have the keys of Hades and of Death." '
(Revelation 1:13–18)

This description of Jesus constitutes the only record of the Lord's physical appearance in the New Testament, and is primarily a symbolic portrait of His Eternal Glory.

The *'garment down to the feet'* bespeaks Messiah's role as High Priest of the New Covenant, Who put away sin by the sacrifice of Himself and forever lives to make intercession for those who come to God by Him (Hebrews 9:26; 7:25).

The *'golden band around the chest'* represents kingship, and thus portrays Messiah as King of kings and Lord of lords, possessing all authority in Heaven and on earth, and enjoying absolute supremacy over every other form of rule, power and dominion (Revelation 19:16; Matthew 28:18; Ephesians 1:20–22).

The *'hair as white as snow'* symbolizes eternalness and wisdom. Messiah is the Eternal Word who was in the beginning with God, and who is the same yesterday, today and forever. Moreover, He is the repository of all wisdom and knowledge, and the embodiment of real truth (John 1:1; Hebrews 13:8; Colossians 2:3; Ephesians 4:21).

The *'eyes of flaming fire'* bespeak Messiah's omniscience. Nothing in creation is hidden from His piercing scrutiny and careful judgment (Hebrews 4:12, 13).

The *'feet like fine brass'* represent Messiah's immutability and omnipotence. He is the all-powerful Lord who changes not (Malachi 3:6; Revelation 19:6).

The *'voice as the sound of many waters'* symbolizes Messiah's majestic strength and commanding authority.

His is the voice that rules over the universal creation (Psalm 29; 33:6, 9).

Messiah holds the *'seven stars in His right hand'* as a poignant symbol of His relationship to the pastors/ messengers of the churches. The Chief Shepherd sustains and protects those whom the Holy Spirit appoints as overseers of the flock of God (1 Peter 5:2–4).

'Out of His mouth proceeds a sharp two-edged sword' thus signifying the awesome power of Messiah's spoken word with which He utterly vanquishes the forces of darkness and strictly governs the affairs of men and nations (Revelation 19:15, 21).

The *'countenance that shines like the sun in its strength'* represents the indescribable glory and majesty of Messiah, who is the radiance of the Father's Glory and the express image of His Person (Hebrews 1:3).

Finally, Messiah is revealed as the Lamb *'who was slain and yet lives'* and is alive forevermore; the One who, by virtue of His death, burial and resurrection is Lord over the realm of death and hell. Through death, Jesus rendered powerless him who had the power of death – the devil – and released those who through fear of death were all their lifetime subject to bondage (Hebrews 2:14, 15).

Messiah Jesus is the *Prince* – the Source, Possessor and Originator – *of Life*. In Him is life and His life is the light of men. By believing that Jesus is Messiah, the Son of God, one may have life in His Name! (Acts 3:15; John 1:4; 20:31).

This is the Jesus who walks among the lampstands – One full of grace and truth, majesty and power. The solemn lesson of this passage is clear: Jesus stands in the midst of His Church in the fullness of His Eternal Glory, waiting to reveal Himself through the power of the Holy Spirit.

He Will Take of Mine

The ministry of the Holy Spirit is to glorify Jesus in the earth. He does this, first of all, by revealing the Glory of Jesus **to** the redeemed, and secondly, by revealing the Glory of Jesus **through** the redeemed to a lost and dying world. The revelation of Jesus in the midst of the Church is the work and pleasure of the Holy Spirit.

> *'However, when He, the Spirit of Truth has come, He will guide you into all truth; for He will not speak on His own authority, but whatever He hears He will speak; and He will tell you things to come. He will glorify Me, for He will take of what is mine and declare it to you. All things that the Father has are Mine. Therefore I said that He will take of Mine and declare it to you.'*
>
> (John 16:13–15)

'Truth' has its frame of reference in the Person and Work of Messiah Jesus. In the words of the Apostle Paul, *'The truth is in Jesus,'* that is, truth centres in, emanates from, and is bounded by the Son of God, who declared Himself to be the embodiment and personification of the 'truth' (Ephesians 4:21; John 14:6). Therefore, 'all truth' constitutes a fuller revelation of the Glory of Jesus.

'He will take of what is Mine,' that is, the Spirit will take of the glorious attributes and excellent virtues of the Messiah, both His nature and power, *'and declare them unto you.'* To emphasize the point, Jesus says, *'All that the Father has is Mine.'* Indeed, the fullness of the Godhead dwells in Him in bodily form (Colossians 2:9). He is the outshining of the Father's Glory and the express image or exact representation of the Father's character (Hebrews 1:3).

Through the ministry of the Holy Spirit, *'Messiah among you, the hope of glory,'* becomes a blessed reality (Colossians 1:27). 'Jesus in the midst,' by the power of the Holy Spirit, is the key that unlocks the door to fullness in the Church.

> *'And He put all things under His feet, and gave Him to be head over all things to the Church, which is His Body, the fullness of Him who fills all in all.'*
>
> (Ephesians 1:22, 23)

The Amplified Bible puts it this way: '*...for in that Body lives the full measure of Him who makes everything complete, and who fills everything everywhere with Himself.*' R.F. Weymouth speaks of the Church as '*the completeness of Him who everywhere fills the universe with Himself.*'

It is not difficult to believe that the fullness of God dwells in Messiah Jesus, but it is a much greater challenge to believe that the fullness of Messiah dwells in the Church. All that Jesus is in Heaven, He is in His Church on earth! God has poured into the Church the fullness of His Son, through the Person of the Blessed Holy Spirit.

Very well. But how does this spiritual fact become experiential reality in the lives of God's people? **Through a consistent and progressive revelation of 'Jesus in the midst' of the redeemed community!**

A case in point is the primitive Church of Jerusalem. The early chapters of the Book of Acts profile this vibrant community of believers, among whom Jesus consistently demonstrated His aliveness and His Lordship by many infallible proofs of grace and power. The fullness of Messiah in this New Testament Church is characterized in the following verses:

> '*Now when they heard this, they were cut to the heart, and said to Peter and the rest of the apostles, "Men and brethren, what shall we do?" Then those who gladly received his word were baptized ... and they continued steadfastly in the apostles' doctrine and fellowship, in the breaking of bread, and in prayers. Then fear came upon every soul, and many wonders and signs were done through the apostles. Now all who believed were together, and had all things in common. And sold their possessions and goods, and divided them among all, as anyone had need. So continuing daily with one accord in the temple, and breaking bread from house to house, they ate their food with gladness and simplicity of heart, praising God and having favour with all the people. And*

> *the Lord added to the Church daily those who were being saved.'* (Acts 2:37, 41–47)

1. Conviction

Jesus is revealed in the convicting power of the Holy Spirit. Conviction is an infallible sign of the presence and ministry of the Holy Spirit, and is the foundation of every genuine spiritual experience and transforming work of grace (John 16:8).

2. Repentance and Obedience

Jesus is revealed in a spirit of repentance and obedience. A change of mind and direction; a complete turning from that which is old, unproductive, carnal, and sinful, and a complete turning to that which is righteous, holy, well-pleasing to God, and new in the Holy Spirit.

Repentance issuing in obedience, is the appropriate preparation for and the proper response to a new manifestation of the Kingdom of God (Matthew 4:17). To Messiah shall be the obedience of the people (Genesis 49:10).

3. The Word of God

Jesus is revealed in the systematic teaching and prophetic preaching of God's Word. The Presence of Jesus catalyses reverence for and submission to the Word.

Moreover, Jesus is the Word (*Logos*), and the anointed exposition of Scripture is, in effect, an unfolding of His Divine Nature and eternal Glory (Luke 24:27; Acts 8:35). Such proclamation undergirds and substantiates the sovereign manifestation of the Holy Spirit.

4. Fellowship and Unity

Jesus is revealed in the fellowship and unity of His Body. The Greek word *'koinonia'*, denotes sharing, unity, partnership, communion, and contributory help. The nature of Messiah, which is unconditional and sacrificial love, is revealed in and demonstrated by the community life of His people (Philippians 2:1–8).

'A new commandment,' said Jesus, *'I give to you, that you love one another, as I have loved you. **By this** all will know that you are My disciples . . . '* (John 13:34, 35).

5. *The Lord's Supper*

Jesus is revealed in the institution of the Lord's Supper. The bread and the wine emblematize the sacrificial death of Jesus on the Cross: His broken body and His shed blood. Believers eat the bread and drink the cup as a 'remembrance and proclamation' of Jesus' death, burial and resurrection.

Each time the Holy Sacrament is celebrated, the Lamb of God is freshly revealed, thus enabling believers to partake in a 'worthy' manner; that is, in appreciation of the full worth of Messiah's redeeming work, as exemplified by the Lord's Supper (1 Corinthians 11:23–29).

The Lord's Supper is therefore, a point of contact for the release of faith – for forgiveness of sin, deliverance from oppression, and healing of sickness.

6. *Prayers*

Jesus is revealed in corporate prayer and intercession. *'If two of you agree on earth concerning anything that they ask, it will be done for them by My Father in Heaven. For where two or three are gathered together in My Name, I am there in the midst of them'* (Matthew 18:19, 20).

The gathering of which Jesus speaks is an assembly of believers engaged in a symphony of prayer. Jesus stands in the midst of such concerts of prayer, to show Himself strong on behalf of those whose hearts are loyal to Him and to do that which is asked in His Name (John 14:13).

Indeed, the House that God lives in is a House of Prayer! (Matthew 21:13).

7. *The Fear of the Lord*

Jesus is revealed in the fear of the Lord, which, in human experience, is a sure sign and a definite proof of the Presence of God. Not cringing apprehension of an unpredictable ogre, but reverential awe of a loving, just and holy Creator (Hebrews 12:28, 29).

In the Bible, men and women commonly responded to the manifest Presence of God by spontaneously prostrating themselves on the ground. This action signalled personal humility and overwhelming veneration for the Glory of God (Revelation 4:8–11).

8. Signs and Wonders

Jesus is revealed in signs, wonders, miracles, and gifts of the Holy Spirit. Contrary to what some may think, such supernatural manifestations do not constitute the primary evidence of Jesus' Presence in the midst of His people.

Nevertheless, signs and wonders are an integral and indispensable proof of the resurrected Messiah. They are God's witnesses – heavenly attestations of the deity and Messiahship of Jesus, and irrefutable evidence of His resurrection from the dead and His Lordship over all creation (Acts 2:22; Hebrews 2:3, 4).

The supernatural work of God, especially in the realm of healing and deliverance, is moreover, a clear revelation and a tangible expression of the nature of Messiah – the kind and gentle Shepherd, who delights in saving that which is lost, curing that which is infirm, and building up that which is destroyed (Isaiah 40:10, 11; John 10:11).

9. Selfless Generosity

Jesus is revealed in selfless generosity and sacrificial giving. *'God so loved the world that He gave . . . '* The nature of God which is love, is personified in the act of giving. The Presence of 'Jesus in the midst' precipitates an outpouring of *agapé* love, resulting in extraordinary acts and attitudes of selfless generosity (Romans 5:5).

The mind or attitude of Messiah is to not hold on to one's position, but to willingly empty oneself of one's privileges for the sake of others; to take the part of a servant, to humble oneself, and to joyfully lay down one's life so that others may live (Philippians 2:5–8).

There is no doubt but that Jesus is in the midst, when this 'mind' becomes the motivating force and governing factor in human relationships.

10. *Gladness and Simplicity*

Jesus is revealed in gladness and simplicity of heart. Joy is an essential part of the nature of God, and for this reason, His Presence inspires joy in the hearts of His people. *'In Your Presence is fullness of joy,'* wrote the Psalmist, and *'at Your right hand are pleasures forevermore'* (Psalm 16:10). When disciples 'see' the Lord with the eye of the Spirit, they rejoice with joy inexpressible and full of glory, which joy is their sustaining strength (John 20:20; 1 Peter 1:8; Nehemiah 8:10).

The complement to godly joy is simplicity of heart. Jesus is revealed in a single, sincere, undivided and unaffected heart. Indeed, *'the eyes of the Lord run to and fro throughout the whole earth, to show Himself strong on behalf of those whose heart is loyal to Him'* (2 Chronicles 16:9).

11. *Praise and Worship*

Jesus is revealed in the praise and worship of His people. God 'inhabits' and is 'enthroned' in the praises of Israel (Psalm 22:3). Praise builds a highway for God to come, by His Spirit, into our personal lives and corporate gatherings. Furthermore, praise builds a house for God to dwell in – an earthly temple for the Heavenly *Shekinah* (Psalm 68:4; Ephesians 2:21, 22).

Where is Jesus to be found today? Hebrews chapter two provides the answer: In the midst of His praising brothers. *'I will declare Your Name to My brethren; in the midst of the assembly I will sing praise to You'* (Hebrews 2:12).

12. *The Church's Growth and Influence*

Jesus is revealed in the consistent growth and expanding influence of His Church. The New Testament concept of church growth does not denote the transfer of members from one congregation to another, but rather, the addition of newly-saved believers. The One who said, *'I will build My Church,'* is Himself revealed in the building thereof, with respect to its numerical strength, spiritual maturity and moral government.

Jesus, in His Church, is the light of the world and the salt of the earth. Jesus, in His Church, is the highly exalted One who draws all men to Himself. Jesus, in His Church, is the King of kings and Lord of lords who rules, spiritually and morally, in the affairs of men and nations (Matthew 5:13–16; 16:18, 19).

Glory in the Church

Jesus is Immanuel, the God who is with us (Matthew 1:23). The Apostle John elaborates on this truth in the first chapter of his gospel:

> *'For out of His fullness (abundance) we all received – all had a share and we were all supplied with – one grace after another and spiritual blessing upon spiritual blessing, and even favour upon favour and gift (heaped) upon gift.'* (John 1:16 Amp.)

Through the New Birth and the Baptism of the Holy Spirit, we receive of Messiah's fullness – each having a unique deposit and a distinct portion. Yet, individually and separately, we cannot hope to fully demonstrate the nature and power of the Lord Jesus. It is only as a united Body, with each member functioning in its God-assigned role in mutual deference and dependence, that we can possibly reveal the fullness of Messiah to the world.

To the corporate Church at Colosse, Paul wrote: *'Messiah among you* (plural)*, the hope of glory!'* (Colossians 1:27). Personal worship and waiting on God is an essential ingredient of spiritual growth, and moreover, lays the foundation for effective corporate gatherings. However, there is a special dynamic of Messiah's Presence available to the corporate gathering which cannot be realized in personal worship. This dynamic is called 'fullness', and is yet another reason why believers should not forsake the assembling of themselves together.

The Apostle Paul referred to this 'special Presence' in 1 Corinthians 5:4;

> *'In the name of our Lord Jesus Christ, when you are gathered together, along with my spirit, with the power of our Lord Jesus Christ.'*

Paul declares that the local church is a gathering together of people into the Name and under the Lordship of Jesus the Messiah, and moreover, **a gathering together with His resurrection power.**

The Greek word *'dunamis'*, translated 'power', denotes 'miraculous power, energy, might, strength, great force, great ability'. Think about it: the *'dunamis'* of the Risen Messiah is present and active in the corporate gathering!

No wonder the Bible records that *'with great power the apostles gave witness to the resurrection of the Lord Jesus,'* and that *'through the hands of the apostles many signs and wonders were done among the people,'* and that *'a multitude gathered from the surrounding cities to Jerusalem, bringing sick people and those who were tormented by unclean spirits, and they were all healed!'* (Acts 4:33; 5:12, 16) This is indeed a description of normal Christian church life.

The Apostle Paul had a Divinely granted understanding of Messiah's fullness in the Church, and of God's determination to reveal that fullness to a watching world:

> *'For this reason I bow my knees to the Father of our Lord Jesus Christ, from whom the whole family in heaven and earth is named, that He would grant you, according to the riches of His glory, to be strengthened with might through His Spirit in the inner man, that Christ may dwell in your hearts through faith; that you, being rooted and grounded in love, may be able to comprehend with all the saints what is the width and*

*length and depth and height – to know the love of Christ
which passes knowledge; that you may be filled with all
the fullness of God. Now to Him who is able to do
exceedingly abundantly above all that we ask or think,
according to the power that works in us, to Him be glory
in the Church by Christ Jesus to all generations, forever
and ever. Amen.'*   (Ephesians 3:14–21)

The personalization of the prayers of Paul is a popular
practice in charismatic circles, and one that I heartily
endorse. However, in so doing, one tends to overlook the
plural tenor of these prayers. In most cases, Paul was
writing to and praying for corporate assemblies rather than
individual believers, for which reason the answer to these
prayers can only be fully realized in a communal dimension.

Consider the expressions of plurality in the above quoted
passage: *'our ... whole family ... your hearts ... all the saints
... we ... us.'* Even the word 'you' is written in a plural form
in the Greek text.

Paul prays for four manifestations of godliness in the
Church at Ephesus. These four should be viewed as different expressions of the one work of grace, rather than as
separate requests.

– **Firstly**, that God would grant them, out of the glorious
riches of His personal resources, which are the perfections of His holy character, to be strengthened with
power by His Spirit in the inner man;
– **Secondly**, that this endowment of glory and power will
be nothing less than Messiah dwelling in their hearts
through faith;
– **Thirdly**, that through the indwelling of Messiah, they
may be deeply rooted and firmly established in love,
which is His essential nature, and may have the power
to grasp the eternal dimensions of that love, understanding it through firsthand experience;
– **Fourthly**, and in summary, that they may be filled up
with all the fullness of God, which is the completeness
of God's own Being.

How can this miracle be realized? The answer is the same as that which was given to Mary by the angel Gabriel: *'The Holy Spirit will come upon you, and the power of the Highest will overshadow you...'* (Luke 1:35). God does infinitely more than we would ever dare to ask or even dream of, **through the power of His Spirit which is at work within us!**

'Glory in the Church' is nothing less than a revelation of 'Jesus in the midst' in all His holiness and majesty – the virtues, perfections, and attributes of the Son of God, reproduced in the lives of His followers. For it is in corporate worship, as the Church gazes upon the glorious Lamb sitting on the Throne, that she is transformed into His image, from glory to glory, the change being effected by the Spirit of the Lord (2 Corinthians 3:18).

Thus, the Church will attain unto the unity of the faith and the full and accurate knowledge of the Son of God, even to mature manhood, which is the full standard of Messiah's own perfection – the completeness that is found in Him (Ephesians 4:13).

'Jesus in the midst' is indeed the Lord's purpose and the Church's destiny.

Chapter 3

Walk in the Spirit

The burden of the Lord for His Church is expressed in the words of the Apostle Paul: *'Walk in the Spirit, and you shall not fulfil the lust of the flesh'* (Galatians 5:16). And again, *'If we live in the Spirit, let us also walk in the Spirit'* (Galatians 5:25).

Walk in the Spirit. Live your whole life habitually in the sphere of the Spirit. Be responsive to and controlled and guided by the Spirit. Let the Spirit direct your course.

The 'Charismatic Renewal' of the 1960s and 70s emphasized the place and work of the Holy Spirit in the life of the individual. However, the Movement of God in the 1990s is emphasizing afresh the place and work of the Holy Spirit in the corporate gathering of the local church.

The appeal to 'Walk in the Spirit' was made, not to individuals *per se*, but to a group of churches in the province of Galatia. It is, in essence, a call to collective spirituality – a corporate walk in the Spirit. The image thus projected is of congregational holiness; a Body of people continually filled with, controlled by and manifesting the attributes of the Spirit of God.

The local Spirit-filled community is the mystery which has been hidden from ages and from generations; God's secret plan which is now being revealed in the earth (Colossians 1:26, 27). For this reason, the local church is, and will always be, the apple of God's eye – the focus of His attention and the object of His affection.

Let us now consider some Old Testament prototypes of communal life in the Spirit.

Tabernacle in the Wilderness

In his testimony to the Sanhedrin, the anointed deacon and first Christian martyr, Stephen, referred to the children of Israel as the 'church' or 'congregation' (Greek: *'ekklesia'*) in the wilderness (Acts 7:38). The journeying of the children of Israel, the ministry of the Tabernacle, the layout of the camp, and the manifestations of God's Presence, were prophetic types of that which was to come in the New Covenant Church.

> *'Now all these things happened to them as examples, and they were written for our admonition, upon whom the ends of the ages have come.'*   (1 Corinthians 10:11)

The Greek word *'tupos'*, translated 'example', denotes 'a die that is struck, a figure formed by a blow, the impress of a seal, a stamp, the pattern in conformity to which a thing must be made, an example to be imitated, a sampler, shape, type, model, an instance of warning'. J.B. Phillips puts it this way: *'Now these things which happened to our ancestors are illustrations of the way in which God works...'*

The Divinely ordered configuration of the Israelite encampment serves as a prophetic model of the New Testament church – the local Spirit-filled community. The centre-piece of the congregation, both geographically and spiritually, was the Tabernacle of Meeting. Housed in the Tabernacle of Meeting, in an area known as the 'Holy of Holies', was the Ark of the Covenant.

> *'And the LORD spoke to Moses and Aaron, saying: "Everyone of the children of Israel shall camp by his own standard, beside the emblems of his father's house;*

they shall camp some distance from the tabernacle of meeting ... And the tabernacle of meeting shall move out with the camp of the Levites in the middle of the camps; as they camp, so they shall move out, everyone in his place, by their standards."' (Numbers 2:1, 2, 17)

More than just a symbolic piece of furniture, the Ark of the Covenant was the actual residence of God's Presence and the seat of God's authority in the camp of Israel. Furthermore, the Ark of the Covenant, with its attendant cherubim, was a copy and a shadow of the Throne of God in Heaven. God commanded Moses to make all things (that is, all things pertaining to the sanctuary), according to the pattern shown him on the mountain (Hebrews 8:5).

Concerning the Tabernacle of Meeting and the Ark of the Covenant, God said:

'And there I will meet with you, and I will speak with you from above the mercy seat, from between the two cherubim which are on the ark of the Testimony, about everything which I will give you in commandment to the children of Israel.' (Exodus 25:22)

'And there I will meet with the children of Israel, and the tabernacle shall be sanctified by My glory ... I will dwell among the children of Israel and will be their God.' (Exodus 29:43, 45)

'... I will appear in the cloud above the mercy seat.' (Leviticus 16:2)

The Ark of the Covenant was the place of God's permanent habitation, not the site of His occasional visitation. Speaking of the Presence of God above the Mercy Seat, the Psalmist declares:

'Give ear, O Shepherd of Israel, You who lead Joseph like a flock; You who dwell between cherubim, shine forth!' (Psalm 80:1)

The Hebrew word *'yashab'*, translated 'dwell', means 'to sit down, remain, settle, marry'. Thus, the Ark of the Covenant was the place where God sat as Judge and ruled as King; the place where He communed with His people as Lord and Lover; and the place of His rest, that is, the home in which He resided. Interestingly, the same Hebrew word is used in Psalm 22:3, where it speaks of God *'inhabiting the praises of Israel.'*

In summary, it was in the Holy of Holies, above the Mercy Seat and between the cherubim, that God **met**, **spoke with**, and **appeared to** Moses and Aaron; the place where His Glory **shone forth** in awesome self-revelation.

The Presence and Glory of God was the centre around which Israel's community life revolved; the focus which gave purpose and meaning to each aspect of Hebrew society. The configuration of the Israelite encampment confirms the essential centrality of the Presence of God in a believing community. Local church life, with its plethora of functions and activities, should likewise revolve around the 'centre' of God's Presence.

The local church can only claim, in truth, to be the House of God, if it is inhabited by the Spirit of God; that is, if there are vital and consistent manifestations of His Presence in the midst. The Book of Revelation and Church history bear joint testimony to a profusion of 'empty' churches like that of Laodicea, where Jesus is on the outside, seeking admittance to the house that bears His name, and 'dying' churches like that of Ephesus, which are in danger of losing the Lamp of God's Presence, and hence, their reason for being.

The House of God is to be a House of Prayer – a community whose chief purpose and main business is communion with God. But how many of us are guilty of turning the Lord's House into a 'den of thieves' – a community whose chief purpose and main business is religious activity! The great deception of religious activity is the notion that the work is an end in itself. In biblical terms, any object or activity which displaces the Presence of God as the centre of life is idolatry, and is worthy of the strictest judgment.

May the Presence of God alone be exalted as the centre of our corporate life and worship. *'The LORD your God in your midst, the Mighty One, will save . . . '* (Zephaniah 3:17).

Pillar of Fire and Cloud

God manifested His Presence to the people of Israel during their journey through the wilderness in the form of a pillar of cloud by day and a pillar of fire by night.

> *'And the LORD went before them by day in a pillar of cloud to lead the way, and by night in a pillar of fire to give them light, so as to go by day and night. He did not take away the pillar of cloud by day or the pillar of fire by night from before the people.'* (Exodus 13:21–22)

Notice that the Bible says, 'the Lord went before them,' and not, 'the Lord followed after them.' Leadership is the prerogative of the Presence of God. In many cases, our prayers for God's blessing are nothing more than pleas for Divine endorsement of humanly conceived initiatives. However, as sheep of the Lord's pasture, we are called to imitate rather than initiate; to follow rather than formulate.

The pillar of cloud led the way and the pillar of fire gave light. God's abiding Presence provided strong leadership for the people of Israel: a sense of clear direction and certain guidance. Furthermore, the Lord's Presence afforded supernatural protection for the whole camp: a sense of security amid the wild beasts and marauding desert tribesmen.

Throughout the Book of Acts, the manifest Presence of God played a central role in the corporate life of local assemblies, whether in Jerusalem, Antioch or Ephesus. In Acts chapter 13, we see the 'Pillar of Cloud' (the Person of the Holy Spirit) going before the congregation at Antioch, leading them along new and unexplored paths of missionary evangelism: *'As they ministered to the Lord and fasted, the Holy Spirit said, "Now separate to Me Barnabas and Saul for the work to which I have called them" ... So, being sent out by the Holy Spirit ... '*

In Acts chapter 4 and 5, we see the 'Pillar of Fire' (the Person of the Holy Spirit) being manifested in the midst of the congregation at Jerusalem, resulting in an overflow of the Grace of God: *'Nor was there anyone among them who lacked; for all who were possessors of lands or houses sold them, and brought the proceeds of the things that were sold, and laid them at the apostles' feet; and they distributed to each as anyone had need.'* Moreover, *'through the hands of the apostles many signs and wonders were done among the people ... and a multitude gathered from the surrounding cities to Jerusalem, bringing sick people and those who were tormented by unclean spirits, and they were all healed.'*

Notice also the constancy of God's Presence in Israel's wilderness journeying: *'He did not take away the pillar of cloud or the pillar of fire from before the people.'* In anti-typical fulfilment of this Old Testament figure, Jesus said to His disciples: *'And I will pray the Father, and He will give you another Helper, that He may abide with you forever ... He dwells with you and will be in you'* (John 14:16, 17).

> *'And the Angel of God, who went before the camp of Israel, moved and went behind them; and the pillar of cloud went from before them and stood behind them. So it came between the camp of the Egyptians and the camp of Israel. Thus it was a cloud and darkness to the one, and it gave light by night to the other, so that the one did not come near the other all that night.'*
>
> (Exodus 14:19, 20)

The pillar of cloud came between the camp of the Egyptians and the camp of Israel. Indeed, the Presence of God is the watershed between the world and the Church, and between those who practise a social Christianity without the life-changing power of the Cross and those who live under the government of the Spirit of God.

The Presence of God validates a congregation of believers. Moses prayed: *'If Your Presence does not go with us, do not bring us up from here. For how then will it be known that Your people and I have found grace in Your sight, except you go with us? So we shall be separate, Your people and I, from all the people who are upon the face of the earth'* (Exodus 33:15, 16). It is the Presence of God which separates Jesus' Church from every other 'church', and it is the Presence of God which is the distinguishing mark of the redeemed community. A true congregation of the Lord is characterized by supernatural manifestations of the Holy Spirit, prompting newcomers to exclaim, *'God is surely in this place!'* (1 Corinthians 14:25).

The mark of God's Presence is an essential element of effective evangelism. When the Lord arises over His people and His Glory is seen upon them, nations will come to their light and kings to the brightness of their rising (Isaiah 60:1–3). In the words of Moses, *'The LORD will establish you as a holy people to Himself ... then all peoples of the earth shall see that you are called by the name of the LORD, and they shall be afraid of you!'* (Deuteronomy 28:9, 10).

> *'Then the cloud covered the tabernacle of meeting, and the glory of the LORD filled the tabernacle. And Moses was not able to enter the tabernacle of meeting, because the cloud rested above it, and the glory of the LORD filled the tabernacle. Whenever the cloud was taken up from above the tabernacle, the children of Israel would go onward in all their journeys. But if the cloud was not taken up, then they did not journey till the day that it was taken up.'* (Exodus 40:34–37)

Herein we see the dominance of the Presence of God. The cloud **covered** and the Glory of the Lord **filled** the tabernacle of meeting. The Hebrew word 'male', translated 'filled', means 'to fill up to the brim or thoroughly saturate'.

When manifested, the Presence of God takes centre stage. Every eye is fixed on the Lord Jesus Christ. God alone is exalted.

The 'weight' of God's Glory leaves no room for human exaltation or fleshly exhibition. Mortal man has nothing to boast of in God's holy Presence (1 Corinthians 1:29). Even Moses, the meekest man on the face of the earth, was not able to enter because of the Glory! He could but prostrate himself in humility and worship before the majesty of God.

Moreover, Israel depended on the initiative of the Presence of God to lead them through the wilderness to the Promised Land. When God's Presence moved forward, the people followed suit, but if God's Presence stood still, the people had no option but to watch and wait. Likewise, the apostles and elders of the Church at Jerusalem put the issue of leadership in proper perspective when they declared, '... *for it seemed good to the Holy Spirit, and to us ...* ' (Acts 15:28).

Such relationship requires a conscious prioritizing of the Presence of God – a recognition that God's Presence is life's most precious possession – and a corresponding sensitivity to and dependence on the indwelling Holy Spirit.

> *'So Moses went out and told the people the words of the Lord, and he gathered the seventy men of the elders of the people and placed them around the tabernacle. Then the Lord came down in the cloud, and spoke to him, and took of the Spirit that was upon him, and placed the same upon the seventy elders; and it happened, when the Spirit rested upon them, that they prophesied, and they did not cease.'* (Numbers 11:24, 25)

The manifestation of God's Presence precipitates an outpouring of the Holy Spirit and a release of the prophetic anointing in the midst of the congregation.

This principle was vividly demonstrated on the Day of Pentecost, AD 32, when the disciples were gathered with one accord in an upper room in Jerusalem. Suddenly there came a sound from heaven, as of a rushing mighty wind, which filled the whole house where they were sitting. Then tongues of fire appeared, resting on each of the disciples. *'And they were all filled with the Holy Spirit and began to speak with other tongues, as the Spirit gave them utterance'* (Acts 2:4).

What were they speaking about? *'... we hear them speaking in our own tongues the wonderful works of God'* (Acts 2:11). The Greek word *'megaleios'*, translated 'wonderful', denotes the 'magnificence, splendour, majesty, sublimity, grandeur, beauty, and excellence of God and His works'. Thus, the disciples spoke prophetically to the nature and power of God in the spiritual realm. Likewise, when the household of Cornelius was filled with the Holy Spirit, they spoke with tongues and magnified God (Acts 10:46).

The 'Pillar of Cloud in the camp of Israel' (the manifest Presence of God in the local church), invariably gives rise to *'psalms, hymns and spiritual songs'* – inspired outpourings of praise, intercession and prophetic utterance (Ephesians 5:18, 19).

> *'Moreover You led them by day with a cloudy pillar, and by night with a pillar of fire, to give them light on the road which they should travel.'*   (Nehemiah 9:12)

The Hebrew word *'or'*, translated 'light', is used both literally and metaphorically. Literally, it denotes a shining light such as that of the sun, and metaphorically it denotes 'life, happiness, favour, salvation and prosperity'.

The priestly blessing of Numbers 6:24 invokes the favour and beneficence of God with these words: *'The LORD bless you and keep you; the LORD make His face shine upon you...'* The manifest Presence of God is a wellspring of life, joy, peace, deliverance and prosperity. *'You will show me the path of life; in Your Presence is fullness of joy; at Your right hand are pleasures forevermore'* (Psalm 16:11).

Another prominent metaphorical usage relates light to **instruction**, and accordingly, to **wisdom and knowledge**. The

Psalmist declared: *'Your Word is a lamp to my feet and a light to my path'* (Psalm 119:105). The 'Pillar of Fire' (the Person of the Holy Spirit), sheds light on the path of the righteous. He guides us into all truth. He teaches us the way in which we should go. He helps us fulfil the will of God. He leads us into the promised land of spiritual inheritance (John 14:26 and 16:13; 1 Corinthians 2:10–12; Ezekiel 36:27).

Remember, these blessings not only pertain to individual believers, but also to congregations that commit themselves to walk as one man in the light of God's Presence. *'O house of Jacob, come and let us walk in the light of the LORD'* (Isaiah 2:5).

> *'Then Miriam and Aaron spoke against Moses because of the Ethiopian woman whom he had married . . . so they said, "Has the LORD indeed spoken only through Moses? Has He not spoken through us also?" And the LORD heard it . . . Suddenly the LORD said to Moses, Aaron, and Miriam, "Come out, you three, to the tabernacle of meeting!" So the three came out. Then the LORD came down in the pillar of cloud and stood in the door of the tabernacle, and called Aaron and Miriam. And they both went forward . . . so the anger of the LORD was aroused against them, and He departed. And when the cloud departed from above the tabernacle, suddenly Miriam became leprous, as white as snow. Then Aaron turned toward Miriam, and there she was, a leper.'*
>
> (Numbers 12:1–2, 4–5, 9–10)

The Lord's Presence brings blessing and comfort to the humble and obedient of His people. But to the self-willed and disobedient, it brings conviction and judgment.

The Presence of God judges between the wheat and the tares, the grain and the chaff, the silver and the dross. The prophet Malachi pictures the Lord coming suddenly to His temple, and then asks, *'But who can endure the day of His coming and who can stand when He appears?'* Why? *'For He is like a refiner's fire and like launderer's soap. He will sit as a refiner and purifier of silver; He will purify the sons of Levi, and purge them as gold and silver . . . I will come near you for judgment; I will be a swift witness . . . '* (Malachi 3:2–5).

The manifest Presence of God separates that which is born of the Spirit and imbued with the Divine Nature from that which is born of the flesh and imbued with self. The Bible uses the illustration of a building engulfed by fire. If the building (one's life and work) is constructed of wood, hay and straw (the attributes of the flesh), it will be utterly destroyed. But if the building is constructed of gold, silver and precious stones (the attributes of God – His Divine nature and character), it will endure and receive a reward (1 Corinthians 3:12–15).

The fire of which the Apostle Paul speaks, is the manifest Presence of God. The Holy Spirit is frequently characterized in Scripture as a consuming fire. In Isaiah 4:4 He is called *'the spirit of judgment and the spirit of burning.'* When the Holy Spirit was poured out on the Day of Pentecost, He appeared as **tongues of fire** on the disciples' heads (Acts 2), and in the Revelation of John He appears as **seven lamps of fire** burning before the Throne of God (Revelation 4:5).

The manifest Presence of God also judges between true and false worship – ministry that is appointed by God and offered in the power of the Spirit, and ministry that is appointed by man and offered in the energy of the flesh. The fire of the Lord can have a devastating affect upon the unqualified and the unprepared, as the impertinent rebel Korah, and his presumptuous colleagues discovered! (Numbers 16).

Revival is the product of a visitation of God and an extraordinary manifestation of His Presence, or as the prophet Malachi puts it, *'the Lord coming suddenly to His temple.'* The density of God's Presence is compounded in times of intense revival. Thus, the Bible speaks of the *'weight of God's Glory.'* The greater the density of God's

Presence, the greater the intensity of revival; the greater the intensity of revival, the swifter the judgment against sin.

In seasons of visitation and revival, God seems to 'draw the reins in' and hold the Church on a very short lead. Thus, sins which may otherwise be tolerated **for a certain time**, are dealt with swiftly and severely.

A case in point is the conspiracy of Ananias and Sapphira in Acts chapter five. The sin of hypocrisy and lying to God has plagued the Church throughout the twenty centuries of her existence, and yet on this occasion the culprits were exposed and struck dead before the whole congregation!

What distinguished this situation from many others of like kind which God apparently tolerated for a longer period of time? The answer is that during seasons of high revival (such as in Acts 5), the holiness of God is more easily offended, the Spirit of God is more easily quenched and the judgment of God is swifter and more severe.

It is indeed a blessed and fearful thing to stand as a congregation in the all-consuming fire of God's manifest Presence.

The Ark of the Covenant

If the calling to succeed Moses as shepherd of Israel was challenging, then the mandate to lead the people into the Promised Land was simply daunting. Thus, it is instructive to note Joshua's utter dependence on the Presence of God, as represented by the Ark of the Covenant.

In the wake of Moses' death, God reassured Joshua with a promise of His Presence: '... *as I was with Moses, so I will be with you. I will not leave you nor forsake you ... Have I not commanded you? Be strong and of good courage; do not be afraid, nor be dismayed, for the* LORD *your God is with you wherever you go'* (Joshua 1:5,9).

The Ark of the Covenant (the Presence of God) played a central role in Israel's crossing of the Jordan and progressive conquest of the Land.

> *'Then Joshua rose early in the morning; and they set out from Acacia Grove and came to the Jordan, he and all the children of Israel, and lodged there before they crossed over. So it was, after three days, that the officers went through the camp; and they commanded the people, saying, "When you see the ark of the covenant of the LORD your God, and the priests, the Levites, bearing it, then you shall set out from your place and go after it. Yet there shall be a space between you and it, about two thousand cubits by measure. Do not come near it, that you may know the way by which you must go, for you have not passed this way before." '*   (Joshua 3:1–4)

Under normal circumstances the Jordan River was about 100 feet wide – tame, shallow and relatively easy to cross. However, at this time of year (April/May, harvest-time), the melting snows of Lebanon and the drenching spring rains caused the river to swell to as much as a mile in width and to flow with a vastly accelerated current. The Jordan River in flood was therefore an impassable barrier which could only be negotiated by supernatural means.

In accordance with Joshua's instructions, the officers commanded the people: *'When you see the Ark of the Covenant being carried forward, then set out from your place and go after it.'* In other words, 'Move with the Presence of God. Don't run ahead and don't lag behind. Walk in the Spirit!' I can almost hear an echo of Moses' cry: 'If Your Presence doesn't go with us, don't take us any further.' After all, who wants to face the raging torrent of the Jordan alone.

Joshua chapter three and verse four contains one of the most important lessons on walking in the Spirit in the whole Bible: *'Yet there shall be a space between you and the Ark of 1,000 yards. Do not come near it, that you may know the way by which you must go, for you have not passed this way before.'*

This is a clear warning against presumption on one hand, and negligence on the other. *'You have not passed this way before.'* You don't know which route to take. You don't know how to ford the river. Acknowledge your utter dependence on the Spirit of God to lead and guide you. And because of this sense of dependency, keep your eyes fixed on the Ark. Stay tuned to the Spirit. Be vigilant – ever listening and watching for the movement of God's Presence.

How reminiscent of Jesus' exhortation to *'watch and pray'* and of the Apostle Paul's instruction to *'keep in step with the Spirit!'* (Luke 21:36; Galatians 5:25)

> *'And Joshua said to the people, "Sanctify yourselves, for tomorrow the LORD will do wonders among you." Then Joshua spoke to the priests, saying, "Take up the Ark of the Covenant and cross over before the people." So they took up the Ark of the Covenant and went before the people. And the LORD said to Joshua, "This day I will begin to exalt you in the sight of all Israel, that they may know that, as I was with Moses, so I will be with you."
> ... And Joshua said, "By this you shall know that the living God is among you, and that He will without fail drive out from before you the Canaanites and the Hittites and the Hivites and the Perizzites and the Girgashites and the Amorites and the Jebusites: Behold the Ark of the Covenant of the Lord of all the earth is crossing over before you into the Jordan."'*
>
> (Joshua 3:5–7, 10–11)

The movement and manifestation of God's Presence summons congregation-wide consecration. *'Pursue holiness,'* declares the epistle to Jewish believers, *'without which no one will see the Lord'* (Hebrews 12:14).

The promise of ever-increasing manifestations of God's Presence calls forth ever-increasing levels of dedication and obedience: *'"I will dwell in them and walk among them. I will be their God, and they shall be My people." ... Therefore, having these promises, beloved, let us cleanse ourselves from all filthiness of the flesh and spirit, perfecting holiness in the fear of God'* (2 Corinthians 6:16b, 7:1).

Another lesson to be learned from this story is that true exaltation does not come from the east or the west – that is, from man or through natural ability – but from the Presence of God.

After successfully encountering and defeating Satan in the wilderness, Jesus *'returned in the power of the Spirit to Galilee, and news of Him went out through all the surrounding region. And He taught in their synagogues, being glorified by all'* (Luke 4:14, 15). Jesus was exalted because He lived, moved and had His being in the Presence of God. He gained a reputation for ministering in the power of the Holy Spirit.

It is the Presence of God that makes one great. It is the Presence of God that makes one strong. It is the Presence of God that gives one authority over demons, disease and death!

Isaiah and Micah prophesied of the exaltation of God's House and the discipling of the nations in the last days. These prophecies began to be fulfilled on the Day of Pentecost when devout Jews from every nation under heaven were drawn by a display of God's power and glory to the fledgling Messianic community.

It was the manifestation of the Spirit that drew people to the House of the Lord in the beginning, and it was the manifestation of the Spirit that continued to draw people to the House of the Lord in the ensuing months and years. Such was the Glory of God in the Church that *'none of the rest dared join them, but the people esteemed them highly, and believers were increasingly added to the Lord, multitudes of both men and women'* (Acts 5:13, 14).

The Presence of God is also the basis for and guarantee of spiritual victory: *'By this you shall know that the living God is among you, and that He will without fail drive out from before you the Canaanites ... Behold, the Ark of the Covenant of the Lord of all the earth is crossing over before you ...'*

When God arises in manifest power and glory, His enemies have no choice but to scatter. Indeed, the wicked perish at the Presence of God (Psalm 68:1, 2). The Spirit of God that is in us is infinitely greater than the spirit of antichrist that is in the world. *'Who can endure the day of Messiah's coming, and who can stand when He appears?'* asked the prophet Malachi. Certainly not the devil or the powers of darkness. The holiness of God is a consuming fire that burns up the chaff of wickedness.

In the Book of Joshua, the book of spiritual conquest, the Holy Ark is called *'The Ark of the Covenant of the Lord of all the earth.'* The Holy Spirit is the Spirit of the Lordship of Jesus. The manifestation of the Spirit reveals the Lordship of Messiah over all of life. His Presence exposes sin, expels demons, heals sicknesses, restores marriages, and makes the circumstances of life conform to the Word and Will of God.

> *'So it was, when the people set out from their camp to cross over the Jordan, with the priests bearing the Ark of the Covenant before the people, and as those who bore the Ark came to the Jordan, and the feet of the priests who bore the Ark dipped in the edge of the water (for the Jordan overflows all its banks during the whole time of harvest), that the waters which came down from upstream stood still, and rose in a heap very far away at Adam, the city that is beside Zaretan. So the waters that went down into the Sea of the Arabah, the Salt Sea, failed, and were cut off; and the people crossed over opposite Jericho. Then the priests who bore the Ark of the Covenant of the* LORD *stood firm on dry ground in the midst of the Jordan; and all Israel crossed over on dry ground, until all the people had crossed completely over the Jordan.'* (Joshua 3:14–17)

In the realm of God's Presence all things are possible. There is no limit to His power; there are no bounds to His might. But the criteria for supernatural activity is the manifestation of His Presence.

Miracles happen in and as a result of the Presence of God. Without His Presence there can be no expectation of the miraculous. Our focus, therefore, should be on the Presence rather than the power! The manifest Presence of God is the active power of God unto salvation in all its various forms.

When my father was in hospital, suffering from a pulmonary embolism that had shattered 75% of his left lung, the Lord Jesus walked into his room and stood at the foot of the bed. Jesus didn't say anything; He just looked at Dad, His eyes full of love and compassion. As Dad, in turn, gazed on the Lord, he began to understand something of the sufferings that Jesus endured on the Cross, as recorded in Psalm 22 and Psalm 88.

Jesus left the room without saying a word, and yet, from that moment on, Dad began to recover, to the amazement and consternation of the doctors. Subsequent x-rays showed that there was not even a trace of scar tissue on the lung that had previously disintegrated! A miracle had taken place. It was the **Presence** of Jesus that made all the difference. It was the **Presence** of Jesus that ministered healing and brought deliverance!

Likewise, it was the Presence of God, represented by the Ark of the Covenant, that caused the waters of the Jordan to stand and rise in a heap (a firm, compact barrier) at the city of Adam, some 16 miles north of the Israelite encampment, thus leaving the river bed dry for a stretch of some 20 to 30 miles, or as far as the eye could see in each direction.

Furthermore, it was the people's faith in and commitment to God's Presence that released the miraculous power of God to work on their behalf. It was when the feet of those who bore the Ark actually dipped in the edge of the water, that the river began to recede.

The message is clear: to follow God's Presence and walk in the Spirit is to walk into a miracle of God's creative power.

The Temple of Solomon

King Solomon is, in many ways, a type of the Lord Jesus Christ. Likewise, the temple that he built in Jerusalem is a figure of the Church that Jesus is building among the nations.

The temple was called 'The House of the Lord,' and as such, was designed to be filled with His manifest Presence. It was not an empty shrine to a far off deity, but a habitation that pulsated with the breath and life of Almighty God! In reference to the temple, God said, *'I have consecrated this house which you have built to put My Name there forever, and My eyes and My heart will be there perpetually'* (1 Kings 9:3).

God's Name represents all the attributes of the Divine Nature – all that God is in the essence of His Being. The expression *'My eyes and My heart'* bespeaks careful attention and loving devotion. In other words, the House of the Lord was to be full of God – His grace and power, holiness and majesty, truth and righteousness.

What a magnificent picture of the Church – God's spiritual house and holy temple – filled with the fullness of Him who fills all things everywhere with Himself!

> *'Then the priests brought in the Ark of the Covenant of the LORD to its place, into the inner sanctuary of the temple, to the Most Holy Place, under the wings of the cherubim ... And it came to pass, when the priests came out of the holy place, that the cloud filled the house of the LORD, so that the priests could not continue ministering because of the cloud; for the glory of the LORD filled the house of the LORD.'*
>
> (1 Kings 8:6, 10, 11)

The Glory of the Lord filled the House of the Lord. This is the Church's *raison d'être*. The House of the Lord is nothing without the Glory of the Lord. The Church is nothing without the fullness of Messiah. As individual believers and local congregations, we are but vessels, waiting to be filled.

There is something wonderful about being interrupted by a visitation of God. Some people decry spontaneous manifestations of the Holy Spirit, but after all, isn't the purpose of our gathering together to meet with God? **The priests could not continue ministering**. The measure of one's willingness to abandon pre-meditated programs in favour of God's new and better (and spontaneous) thing is the measure of one's hunger for the Glory of God.

I think that sometimes we leaders are more concerned about holding on to our authority than we are of seeing a manifestation of God's Power and Glory. As God begins to move, the leadership in a certain sense passes out of our hands, and we, along with the rest of the congregation, have to bow before His Majesty. This is the real meaning of 'waiting on God' – relinquishing our right to rule and desire to control in deference to the Sovereignty of the Holy Spirit.

The Apostle Peter was tested on this very point while ministering to the Gentiles in Cornelius' house. Halfway through his sermon, *'the Holy Spirit fell upon all those who heard the Word, and they spoke with tongues and magnified God'* (Acts 10:44, 46). Such an outburst was certainly not on the program. However, Peter had the good sense to stand aside and let God have His way.

The Glory of God, when revealed, fills the house. The Presence of God, when manifested, transcends everything and everyone else. God must increase and man must decrease.

The hallmark of a true movement of the Spirit is the exaltation of Jesus, and Him alone. *'Enter into the rock, and hide in the dust, from the terror of the LORD and the glory of His majesty. The lofty looks of man shall be humbled, the haughtiness of men shall be bowed down, and the LORD alone shall be exalted in that day'* (Isaiah 2:10, 11). Amen! May all true servants of the Lord cry, *'Even so, come Lord Jesus!'*

They were all filled

The fourth chapter of Acts contains a promise of things to come for the redeemed community of the last days. It is a picture of a Church under siege, which, in its distress, calls upon the Lord for spiritual power and supernatural boldness. Moreover, it is a revelation of God's will and purpose for His people, as seen in the congregation-wide outpouring of the Holy Spirit.

> *'And being let go, they went to their own companions and reported all that the chief priests and elders had said to them. So when they heard that, they raised their voice to God with one accord and said: "Lord, You are God ... Now Lord, look on their threats, and grant to Your servants that with all boldness they may speak Your Word, by stretching out Your hand to heal, and that signs and wonders may be done through the name of Your holy Servant Jesus." And when they had prayed, the place where they were assembled together was shaken; and they were all filled with the Holy Spirit, and they spoke the Word of God with boldness.'*
>
> (Acts 4:23, 24a, 29–31)

In my years of ministry I have witnessed numerous outpourings of the Holy Spirit – God touching individuals, and in some cases, sections of a congregation with His Presence and Glory. But the best is yet to come!

God wants to visit the corporate gatherings of His people and change every life, meet every need, cleanse every sin, heal every sickness and imbue everyone present with a deeper revelation of the Glory of the Lord. God wants to fill entire congregations with His Holy Spirit, **at the one time**.

The precedent for mass outpourings of the Holy Spirit and aggregable demonstrations of the power of God was established in the ministry of Jesus: *'At evening, when the sun had set, they brought to Him all who were sick and those who were demon-possessed. And the whole city was gathered together at the door. Then He healed many who were sick with various diseases, and cast out many demons . . . '* (Mark 1:32–34)

And again, in Luke 4:40–41; *'When the sun was setting, all those who had any that were sick with various diseases brought them to Him; and He laid His hands on every one of them and healed them. And demons also came out of many, crying out and saying, "You are the Christ, the Son of God!"'*

Several years ago, in an issue of *Abundant Life* magazine, Reverend Oral Roberts shared some insights the Lord had given him concerning the end-time ministry. One point in particular stands out in my mind.

Brother Roberts predicted that on some occasions the Holy Spirit would come into corporate gatherings like a rushing mighty wind and blow upon the congregation. And in His wake, every sinner in the house would be saved, every sick person would be healed, and every hungry soul would be filled with the Glory of God. Brother Roberts went on to say that in all the years of his crusade ministry, this had only occurred three times. But he predicted that in the coming revival, visitations such as this would increase in frequency and commonality.

I believe with all my heart that in the days to come we shall see Pentecost revisited: when two or three, or two or three thousand are gathered together in one accord in one place under the Lordship of Jesus, and suddenly there comes a sound from heaven as of a rushing mighty wind, and the manifest Presence of God fills the room in which the believers are gathered, satiating the spirit, mind and body of everyone present!

Chapter 4

Anointing Jesus as Head of the Church

We will never achieve any kind of spiritual maturity unless we first come to grips with the preeminence of the Lord Jesus Christ.

The word 'maturity' connotes a certain decentralization of self. Newborn babies, in their winsome innocence, are totally self-centred. And woe to the person who begrudges their tiny demands! But as the infant passes through the progressive stages of childhood development, he or she is expected (with the help of godly training and discipline) to lose much of the selfish instinct.

There is nothing more detestable than a selfish child, not to mention a self-centred teenager, and, Heaven forbid, a self-centred adult! Maturity is, in essence, coming to grips with the 'bigger picture' of life in which 'I' am no longer the centre around which the universe revolves.

Spiritual maturity is recognizing Jesus as the Centre of all things, and ordering one's life accordingly. *'He died for all, that those who live should live no longer for themselves, but for Him who died for them and rose again'* (2 Corinthians 5:15). God takes pleasure in the prosperity of His people (Psalm 35:27). His chief joy, however, is in the exaltation of His Son.

> *'Therefore God also has highly exalted Him and given Him the Name which is above every name, that at the*

Name of Jesus every knee should bow, of those in heaven, and of those on earth, and of those under the earth, and that every tongue should confess that Jesus Christ is Lord, to the glory of God the Father.'

(Philippians 2:9–11)

The universal acclamation of the Son becomes an anthem of praise, worship and honour to the Father. There is no competition in the Godhead. Indeed, *'it pleased the Father that in Him all the fullness should dwell'* (Colossians 1:19).

The Greek word *'eudokeo'*, translated 'pleased', casts an interesting light on the disposition of the Father toward the Son. *'Eudokeo'* signifies 'to be well pleased' or 'to think it good'. The word stresses 'the willingness and freedom of an intention or resolve regarding what is good'. Thus, the New English Bible speaks of the complete being of God coming to dwell in the Son **by God's own choice!**

'He is the image of the invisible God, the firstborn over all creation. For by Him all things were created that are in heaven and that are on earth, visible and invisible, whether thrones or dominions or principalities or powers. All things were created through Him and for Him. And He is before all things, and in Him all things consist. And He is the Head of the body, the church, who is the beginning, the first born from the dead, that in all things He may have the preeminence.'

(Colossians 1:15–18)

Jesus is the exact revelation and representation of the invisible God, and the 'firstborn' over all creation. The title of 'firstborn' refers to Jesus' exalted position, that is, His priority to and preeminence over all creation. In Jewish society, a firstborn son was endowed with great privilege and responsibility. Thus, Jesus is declared to be the Head of the Father's household, the appointed heir and lawful owner of all things.

The title of 'firstborn' bears no reference whatsoever to

the timing of Jesus' physical birth, nor does it in any way imply a commencement of spiritual existence in the sense of being 'born' or 'created'. Jesus is the Eternal Son who always was, always is and always will be. He is the absolutely pre-existent One who rules over all creation; the Creator, Sustainer and Goal of all things; the Centre in which the whole universe coheres.

The eternal purpose of God is summed up in these words: *'that in all things He may have the preeminence.'* The Greek word *'proteuo'*, translated 'pre-eminence', means 'to be first'. R.F. Weymouth says, *'that He might occupy the foremost place.'* The New English Bible puts it this way: *'to be in all things alone supreme.'* And the Living Bible, *'so that He is first in everything.'*

The Apostle Paul speaks of the eternal purpose of God being **centred** and **realized** in Christ Jesus the Lord (Ephesians 3:11). And with great eloquence, he elaborates on the one great goal of the universe:

> *'Having made known to us the mystery of His will, according to His good pleasure which He purposed in Himself, that in the dispensation of the fullness of the times He might gather together in one all things in Christ, both which are in heaven and which are on earth – in Him. In Him also we have obtained an inheritance, being predestined according to the purpose of Him who works all things according to the counsel of His will.'*
>
> (Ephesians 1:9–11)

'Oikonomia', the Greek word translated 'dispensation', primarily signifies 'the management of a household or of household affairs'. It bespeaks 'administration, oversight, government and stewardship'. Thus, a 'dispensation' is not a period or epoch, but 'a mode of dealing, an arrangement or administration of affairs'.

The dispensation of which Paul speaks is none other than the government of God, resting upon the shoulders of His

Beloved Son. The consummation of all things in Messiah. The uniting of the whole universe under His Headship!

Listen to R.F. Weymouth's translation, and then compare it with that of the Twentieth Century New Testament:

> '*For the government of the world when the times are ripe for it – the purpose which He has cherished in His own mind of restoring the whole creation to find its one Head in Christ.*'

> '*In view of that Divine Order which was to mark the completion of the ages, when He should make everything ... centre in Him.*'

In accordance with this purpose, we have become God's inheritance and have ourselves obtained an inheritance!

Our inheritance is bound up with the inheritance of the Son. Through the instrumentality of the Church, Messiah will come into the fullness of His inheritance, and through the accession of Messiah, the Church will come into the fullness of her inheritance.

The Head and the Body

The Apostle Paul employs a variety of metaphors to describe the rich and multifaceted relationship of Messiah Jesus and His Church, the most widely quoted of which is 'the body'.

The human body is a classic study in organic unity and integrated wholeness: '*Our bodies have many parts, but the many parts make up only one body when they are all put together. So it is with the "body" of Christ. Each of us is a part of the one body of Christ...*' (1 Corinthians 12:12, 13 TLB).

The relationship of Jesus to His Church is like that of a head to a body – an inseparable union and a total identification. '*Abide in Me, and I in you...*' (John 15:4), and '*He*

who is joined to the Lord is one spirit with Him'
(1 Corinthians 6:17). Moreover, the position of 'Head'
signifies Messiah's absolute preeminence in all things
pertaining to the Church.

> *'And He put all things under His feet, and gave Him to*
> *be head over all things to the Church, which is His body,*
> *the fullness of Him who fills all in all.'*
>
> (Ephesians 1:22,23)

The 'head' is the command and control centre that
dictates the behaviour of the body in general, and each
member in particular. Decisions are made by the head and
implemented by the body. Directions are given by the head
and followed by the body. The prerogative of initiative
belongs to the head, and the head alone.

When a member of the body loses contact with the head
and no longer responds to its commands, that member is
referred to as being **dead** or **numb**. And when the head loses
contact with and control over the rest of the body and the
parts thereof act in an independent and uncoordinated
fashion, the victim is said to be suffering from **cerebral
palsy** or some other kindred disease.

Thanks to God, there is a cure for cerebral palsy and
every other kind of sickness and disease: *'He Himself took
our infirmities and bore our sicknesses, and by His stripes we
were healed'* (Matthew 8:17; 1 Peter 2:24). But is there a
cure for the spiritual disease that is crippling the Body of
Messiah – the disease of 'not maintaining vital union with
the Head?'

> *'And not holding fast to the Head, from whom all the*
> *body, nourished and knit together by joints and liga-*
> *ments, grows with the increase that is from God.'*
>
> (Colossians 2:19)

What is the greatest challenge facing the Church? The
call to evangelize the world? The call to overcome the

powers of darkness? Or the call to be subject to Messiah in all things. Listen friends, submission is the greatest challenge, but it also yields the greatest reward!

Submission, then Fullness

Ephesians chapter five paints a beautiful picture of the love relationship between Jesus and the Church, as reflected on the human plane in Christian marriage and family.

> *'Wives, submit to your own husbands, as to the Lord. For the husband is the head of the wife, as also Christ is head of the church; and He is the Saviour of the body. Therefore, just as the church is subject to Christ, so let the wives be to their own husbands in everything. Husbands, love your wives, just as Christ also loved the church and gave Himself for her, that He might sanctify and cleanse her with the washing of water by the Word, that He might present her to Himself a glorious church, not having spot or wrinkle or any such thing, but that she should be holy and without blemish.'*

(Ephesians 5:22–27)

The Greek word *'hupotasso'* appears some 41 times in the New Testament, and is variously translated 'subject, submit, put under, subdue', and 'be obedient to'. The word literally means to 'stand under'.

Submission is the voluntary placing of oneself under Divinely ordered authority – the volitional action of 'standing under' God's appointed representatives. Thus, submission is first an attitude, then an action. *'If you are willing and obedient ... but if you refuse and rebel'* (Isaiah 1:19, 20). A willing spirit issues in acts of obedience. But a proud and defiant heart expresses itself in acts of rebellion. *'A good man out of the good treasure of his heart brings forth good things, and an evil man out of the evil treasure brings forth evil things'* (Matthew 12:35).

Submission cannot be coerced. The Bible does not say,

'Make others submit to you,' but rather, 'submit your-self...' We are called to voluntarily subject ourselves to Messiah **in all things**; to humble ourselves under God's mighty hand; to stand under His authority and embrace His rulership by praying, *'Your Kingdom come, Your will be done.'*

The Church's recognition of Messiah's Headship enables Him to function as 'Saviour' of the Body in the fullest sense of the word. (The Greek word *'soter'* signifies a 'deliverer, preserver, saviour, benefactor', and 'rescuer'). Further-more, the Church's subjection of herself to Messiah in all things enables Him to sanctify and cleanse her with the washing of water by the Word, to the end that she may be a glorious Church, or a Church full of glory, not having spot or wrinkle or any such thing, but entirely holy and without blemish!

Consider the following equation:

the deeper the subjection, the more thorough the wash-ing; and the more thorough the washing, the greater the glory that is revealed!

It is as the Church submits to Messiah that she is cleansed by His Word, transformed into His image, and filled with His fullness. It is through our abiding in Him that He abides in us.

'And He put all things under His feet, and gave Him to be head over all things to the Church, which is His body, the fullness of Him who fills all in all.'

(Ephesians 1:22, 23)

The manifestation of Messiah's fullness in the Church is commensurate with the Church's acknowledgement of His Headship. Messiah fills whosoever and whatsoever is submitted to Him. His Glory is revealed within the sphere of His authority. For this reason, *'God inhabits the praises of Israel,'* that is, His Presence is manifested in the lives of people who love Him with all their heart, soul, mind and strength – people whose lives are wholly dedicated to Him.

The more the Church comes under Messiah's actual rule, the greater will be the manifestations of His Presence and Glory in her midst.

> *'He who descended is also the One who ascended far above all the heavens, that He might fill all things. And He Himself gave some to be apostles, some prophets, some evangelists, and some pastors and teachers, for the equipping of the saints for the work of ministry, for the edifying of the body of Christ, till we all come to the unity of the faith and the knowledge of the Son of God, to a perfect man, to the measure of the stature of the fullness of Christ.'* (Ephesians 4:10–13)

Apostles, prophets, evangelists, pastors and teachers are gifts of Messiah to the Church – diverse expressions and complimentary manifestations of His Presence, Power and Glory. *'To each one us grace was given according to the measure of Christ's gift'* (Ephesians 4:7), and *'from His abundance we have all had a share'* (John 1:16 Gdspd). There are diversities of gifts, differences of ministries, and diversities of activities, but they are all expressions of the One Spirit, the One Lord, and the One God (1 Corinthians 12:4–6).

The Church must view the ministry gifts, and more importantly, the ministry gifts must view themselves, in the light of God's declared purpose: *'He who went down is the same as He who went up – up beyond the highest heaven, that He might fill all things with His Presence'* (TCNT), or as J.B. Phillips puts it, *'that the whole universe from lowest to highest might know His Presence.'* The ministry gifts are means to an end – the end being the supreme exaltation of Messiah and the universal manifestation of His Glory.

In order for an apostle to fully realize his apostleship and a prophet to fully apprehend his prophetic calling etc., the revelation of Messiah must become his single passion and goal. Beware: mixed motives produce half-baked ministers.

Anointing Jesus

The Hebrew word *'Mashach'*, translated 'anoint', means 'to rub or smear with oil, especially in order to consecrate someone or something'. The practice of anointing with oil signifies the calling out and setting apart of people and things for sacred service. Thus, anointing bespeaks Divine ownership and destiny.

Furthermore, the anointing is a symbol of the Presence and Power of the Holy Spirit in the life of the 'called out' one. It bespeaks Divine empowerment – an investiture of authority and power for service.

The kings of Israel were installed in office by the rite of anointing. Saul, David and Solomon are specifically referred to as *'the Lord's anointed'* (Hebrew: *'mashiach'* – 'messiah').

The ancient seers of Israel, however, prophesied of a Messiah who would outrank all others ... possessing all authority, power, wisdom and strength ... whose anointing excelled that of His brethren – Jesus of Nazareth, the Son of the Living God!

The Lord Jesus possesses all authority in heaven and on earth. He is seated in strength and majesty at the Father's right hand, far above all rule, authority, power, dominion and title of sovereignty, not only in this age but also in that which is to come. He is crowned with many crowns of glory, honour and power. He is altogether lovely, altogether holy, and altogether wonderful. He is exalted to the place of highest honour in Heaven, and His Glory fills the whole universe.

Why, then, is the Church called to exalt One who is already so highly exalted? And how can the Church anoint One who is already so lavishly anointed? And how can the Church possibly crown One who already possesses all authority in heaven and on earth?

The answer is found in what is commonly known as 'The Lord's Prayer', but is in actual fact 'The disciples' Kingdom prayer'.

> *'Our Father in heaven, hallowed be Your name. Your kingdom come. Your will be done on earth as it is in heaven.'* (Matthew 6:9, 10)

The Kingdom of God is an established fact. Jesus has risen from the dead and is Lord over all. We don't have to pray for it to happen – it has happened and is forever settled in Heaven! God is in full control; Jesus is highly exalted; and the devil is totally defeated. Hallelujah! Nothing that man does can add to or take away from the reality of Messiah's Lordship. The rule of God is absolute.

And yet, in this seat of rebellion and lawlessness called Earth, in this theatre of conflict between the forces of Heaven and Hell, the rule of God is challenged and the preeminence of the Son is denied, albeit futilely and for a very short time.

'Your Kingdom come' is explained in the following, *'Your will be done on earth as it is in heaven.'* In other words, let life on Earth conform to the order and quality of life in Heaven. The 'Kingdom Prayer' is a prayer of alignment – of Earth with Heaven. It's not a matter of 'may Jesus become Lord,' but rather, 'may the nations recognize that He is Lord, and behave accordingly.'

Thus, the call to *'exalt the Lord, anoint the Son, and crown the King'* is a call to acknowledge and embrace that which God has already done in the Person of Messiah Jesus. We cannot make Jesus 'Lord' anymore than we can make God 'God' – but we can confess His Lordship, bow our knee to His Sovereignty, and accept the yoke of His discipline.

To anoint Jesus as Head of the Church is to work out His Lordship in practical day to day living – by following the leading of His Spirit, submitting to the authority of His Word, and honouring the representative levels of His government (e.g. parents–children, husbands–wives, pastors–churches, rulers–people).

Anointing the Church

The anointing of Jesus as Head of the Church through prayer, worship, love and obedience is not the end of the story, but the beginning. Indeed, it sets off a chain reaction in the Body which can only be described as spiritual fullness and overflowing life.

> *'Behold, how good and how pleasant it is for brethren to dwell together in unity! It is like the precious oil upon the head, running down on the beard, the beard of Aaron, running down on the edge of his garments. It is like the dew of Hermon, descending upon the mountains of Zion; for there the* LORD *commanded the blessing – life forevermore.'* (Psalm 133)

The Book of Ephesians teaches us that the unity of the Church and of all creation is bound up in the Headship of Jesus: *'the summing up of all things in Christ,'* or *'the uniting of the whole creation under His headship'* (Ephesians 1:10). And again in chapter four and verse fifteen: *'But, speaking the truth in love, may grow up in all things into Him who is the Head – Christ.'*

The High Priestly prayer that our Lord offered up at the conclusion of the *Pesach* meal, just prior to His arrest in Gethsemane, centres on this principle: *'That they all may be one, as You, Father, are in Me, and I in You; that they also may be one in Us, that the world may believe that You sent Me'* (John 17:21).

As we all, with one accord, turn our eyes upon Jesus and allow Him to take His rightful place as Head, a veritable revolution will take place in the Church: the fullness of the Head – all that Jesus is and has; His nature and power, character and ability – will permeate the Body, so as to make Ephesians 1:23 a blessed reality.

The New Testament refers to the Church as *'the body of the Anointed One'* (1 Corinthians 12:27), or to put it another way, *'the Anointed Body.'* The Anointing that rests upon the Head flows over the beard, the shoulders, the chest, the loins, and down to the feet. The fullness of the Spirit that has been given to Jesus in Heaven is poured out upon His Church on Earth.

> *'Therefore being exalted to the right hand of God, and having received from the Father the promise of the Holy Spirit, He poured out this which you now see and hear.'*
> (Acts 2:33)

God anointed Jesus of Nazareth with the Holy Spirit and with power, and in the strength of that anointing He went about doing good, and healing all who were oppressed of the devil (Acts 10:38). After His resurrection, Jesus appeared to his disciples and said to them, *'As the Father has sent Me, I also send You.'* And breathing on them, He said, *'Receive the Holy Spirit'* (John 20:21, 22).

The Anointing that rests upon Jesus, also rests upon the Church. The fullness of the Head fills the whole Body. As stated in Psalm 133, this congregation-wide outpouring, corporate fullness, and bodily anointing is the blessing of life – God's Life – in superabundant measure!

Saul and David

The inaugural king of Israel, Saul, commenced his reign as the Lord's anointed and ended his reign as the Lord's rejected. The essence of Saul's disqualification was his refusal to accept the government of God, evidenced by his disobedience to the Word of the Lord, given expressly by the prophet Samuel.

> *'And Samuel said to Saul, "You have done foolishly. You have not kept the commandment of the LORD your God, which He commanded you. For now the LORD*

> *would have established your kingdom over Israel forever.*
> *But now your kingdom shall not continue. The LORD has*
> *sought for Himself a man after His own heart, and the*
> *LORD has commanded him to be commander over His*
> *people, because you have not kept what the LORD*
> *commanded you."'* (1 Samuel 13:13, 14)

Because of his infatuation with his own authority, Saul forgot the Lord, the Most High God and the ultimate Ruler of Israel. Moreover, Saul's respect for man and desire for human affirmation eclipsed his reverence for God and any desire he might have had to please Him.

> *'So Samuel said: "Has the LORD as great delight in*
> *burnt offerings and sacrifices, as in obeying the voice of*
> *the LORD? Behold, to obey is better than sacrifice, and to*
> *heed than the fat of rams. For rebellion is as the sin of*
> *witchcraft, and stubbornness is as iniquity and idolatry.*
> *Because you have rejected the word of the LORD, He also*
> *has rejected you from being king." Then Saul said to*
> *Samuel, "I have sinned, for I have transgressed the*
> *commandment of the LORD and your words, because I*
> *feared the people and obeyed their voice."'*
> (1 Samuel 15:22–24)

The Word of the Lord is a tangible expression of His authority and a manifest token of His Lordship. To reject the Word of the Lord is to rebel against the rule of God. *'Because you have rejected the Word of the Lord, He also has rejected you from being king.'* If one is to reign with Messiah, one must first submit to Messiah.

> *'And when He had removed him (Saul), He raised up for*
> *them David as king, to whom also He gave testimony and*
> *said, "I have found David the son of Jesse, a man after*
> *My own heart, who will do all My will."'* (Acts 13:22)

David, Saul's successor, is described as *'a man after God's own heart.'* What is the definition of a man after God's heart? One who wills to do the will of God. One who acknowledges the preeminence and submits to the Lordship of God's Anointed.

The attitude of David's heart is most clearly revealed in Psalm 23: 'The Lord is my Shepherd, I shall not want. He makes me to lie down ... He leads me ... He restores my soul ... He comforts me ... He prepares a table before me ... He anoints my head ... I will dwell in His house forever.'

Can you see the emphasis? The Lord leads and the Lord feeds! The Lord guides and the Lord provides! Psalm 23 is a case of 'follow the leader'. It is the heart-cry of a man who delights in the government of God – one who happily submits to the rule of the King.

And it was to David that the Lord turned after the débâcle of Saul. To the young man, who, through pure love, whole-hearted devotion, courageous obedience, and exultant praise, exalted God's Beloved as Lord, anointed God's Chosen as Head, and crowned God's Appointed as King. Of this man, God said, *'I have provided and seen for Myself a king.'* And when he stood before the prophet Samuel,

> *'Samuel took the horn of oil and anointed him in the midst of his brothers; and the Spirit of the LORD came upon David from that day forward ...'*
>
> (1 Samuel 16:13)

May the disposition of the Church toward her Head be like that of David toward his Shepherd-Lord. And by virtue of that disposition, may she be anointed with a horn of fresh oil to rule and reign with Messiah the King.

Chapter 5

Blessed Are the Pure in Heart

The primary qualification for seeing the Glory of God is holiness, or purity of heart. The Book of Hebrews exhorts us to *'pursue peace with all people, and holiness, without which no one will see the Lord'* (Hebrews 12:14).

The Greek word *'hagiasmos'*, translated 'holiness', signifies 'separation from sin and consecration to God'. It denotes both the **process** of sanctification – the inauguration and maintenance of a life of fellowship with God – and the **resultant state** of sanctification, in which one's life is wholly devoted to God and perfectly conformed to His image. Thus, holiness is actually 'wholeheartedness' as expressed in the *Shema*: *'You shall love the LORD your God with all your heart, with all your soul, and with all your strength'* (Deuteronomy 6:5).

It is precisely this kind of wholeheartedness which enables one to see the Glory of God. **Separation** (coming out of the world system, Babylon; turning from sin; putting away idols) and **dedication** (an unreserved embracing of God and His ways) is the only basis on which God can manifest His Presence and reveal His Glory in the midst of His people.

The Apostle Paul argued this point in 2 Corinthians, chapters six and seven:

> *'Do not be unequally yoked together with unbelievers. For what fellowship has righteousness with lawlessness?*

And what communion has light with darkness? And what accord has Christ with Belial? Or what part has a believer with an unbeliever? And what agreement has the temple of God with idols? For you are the temple of the living God. As God has said: "I will dwell in them and walk among them. I will be their God, and they shall be My people." Therefore "Come out from among them and be separate, says the Lord. Do not touch what is unclean, and I will receive you. I will be a Father to you and you shall be My sons and daughters, says the LORD Almighty." Therefore, having these promises, beloved, let us cleanse ourselves from all filthiness of the flesh and spirit, perfecting holiness in the fear of God.'

(2 Corinthians 6:14–7:1)

A Matter of the Heart

Whilst holiness has very much to do with one's behaviour and appearance, it is first and foremost a matter of the heart.

Holiness represents the attitude of one's heart toward sin and the world system on one hand, and God and His Kingdom on the other. Holiness is a burning hatred of sin and a despising of unrighteousness, and at the same time, an intense love for the Person and character of God, and a delighting in His righteousness.

King David was a man who saw the Glory of God revealed in his life and circumstances. The key to David's spiritual success was his wholehearted approach to God. Consider the following statements:

'I will praise You, O LORD, with my whole heart.'

(Psalm 9:1)

'Blessed are those ... who seek Him with the whole heart.' (Psalm 119:2)

'With my whole heart I have sought you.'

(Psalm 119:10)

'... *I shall observe it* (Your Law) *with my whole heart.'*
(Psalm 119:34)

'I entreated Your favour with my whole heart...'
(Psalm 119:58)

'... *I will keep Your precepts with my whole heart.'*
(Psalm 119:69)

'I cry out with my whole heart; Hear me, O LORD*!'*
(Psalm 119:145)

'Teach me Your way, O LORD*; I will walk in Your truth;
Unite my heart to fear Your Name. I will praise You, O*
LORD *my God, with all my heart, and I will glorify Your
Name forevermore.'* (Psalm 86:11–12)

Notice the cry of David in Psalm 86, *'Unite my heart.'*
Other translations read, *'Give me singleness of heart,'* or
'Give me an undivided heart.' Elsewhere, David asks God to
give Him a 'clean' or 'pure' heart. Once again, the concept
is of a heart that is entirely composed of one substance –
unsullied, unadulterated, without admixture, free from
contamination.

Holiness is having eyes for Jesus alone; it is laying up
treasure in Heaven; it is setting one's mind and affection on
things above, not on things on the earth; it is seeking first
the Kingdom of God; in short, it is having no other god
but the Lord.

The hopelessness of admixture is revealed in these words:
*'No one can serve two masters; for either he will hate the one
and love the other, or else he will be loyal to the one and
despise the other. You cannot serve God and materialism'*
(Matthew 6:24). Divided loyalty is not only sinful; it is
downright impractical. Indeed, *'if anyone loves the world,
the love of the Father is not in him'* (1 John 2:15).

God's Search

During the course of conversation with the woman at the

well, Jesus declared that *'the Father is seeking true worshippers who will worship Him in spirit and truth'* (John 4:23), or to put it another way, *'people who will draw near to Him with sincere hearts in fulness of faith'* (c.p. Hebrews 10:22). A similar statement was made by the prophet Hanani in 2 Chronicles 16:9;

> *'For the eyes of the LORD run to and fro throughout the whole earth, to show Himself strong on behalf of those whose heart is loyal to Him.'*

What kind of person is God searching for? One whose heart is loyal ... wholly devoted ... fully persuaded ... totally committed. God delights in the characteristic of wholeheartedness and prizes it above all else. And it is to people like this that God shows Himself strong. He yearns to make His Presence known to His consecrated ones: *'To the saints God wills to make known the riches of the glory of Messiah in the midst of His Church'* (Colossians 1:27).

The Lord certainly knows those who are His (2 Timothy 2:19). The Word of God judges the very thoughts and intents of the heart, and no created thing is able to escape its scrutiny. Everything lies bare and completely exposed before the eyes of Him to Whom we must give account (Hebrews 4:12, 13). As the Lord said to Samuel, *'Man looks at the outward appearance, but the Lord looks at the heart'* (1 Samuel 16:7). *'All the ways of a man are pure in his own eyes, but the LORD weighs the spirits and tests the motives'* (Proverbs 16:2).

How well do we know God and how much of His counsel do we proclaim? The Apostle Paul said, *'Consider the goodness **and** severity of God'* (Romans 11:22). The Lord is a God of truth and justice who scrutinizes **everything**, especially the hearts of His people. The writer to the Hebrews highlighted this often neglected facet of the Divine Nature:

> *'For we know Him who said, "Vengeance is Mine, I will repay," says the Lord. And again, "The LORD will judge*

> *His people.'' It is a fearful thing to fall into the hands of*
> *the Living God.'* (Hebrews 10:30–31)

God is more concerned with our motives and attitudes than He is with our behaviour, because in the final analysis, the external merely reflects the internal. *'As a man thinks in his heart, so is he'* (Proverbs 23:7), and, *'out of the heart proceed evil thoughts, murders, adulteries, fornications, thefts, false witness, blasphemies'* (Matthew 15:19).

During his exile on the Isle of Patmos, John received a revelation of the Lord Jesus as the glorified Son of Man; Prophet, Priest and King; Messiah, Redeemer and Judge; Whose head and hair were white like wool and Whose eyes were like a flame of fire.

The 'eye' is the faculty of omniscience with which the Lord searches the hearts and minds of His people. 'Fire' bespeaks judgment and purification. Thus, the Lord Jesus is revealed as One who scrutinizes our motives and attitudes in order to cleanse us from every defilement and contaminating influence, and present us to God 'a whole burnt offering,' a holy living sacrifice.

> *'. . . and all the churches shall know that I am He*
> *who searches the minds and hearts. And I will give*
> *to each one of you according to your works.'*
> (Revelation 2:23)

The Lord searches people's minds and hearts. He tests motives and judges attitudes. He deals with us **primarily** on the basis of what we want to be and do – that is, according to our motives and desires – rather than on the basis of what we presently have and are. If we persist, God will eventually give us the desires of our heart, but beware, if our 'eye' (motive, desire) is 'bad' (evil, unhealthy), our whole 'body' (life) will be full of darkness (Matthew 6:23). The granting of such desires brings leanness to one's soul (Psalm 106:15).

Therefore, it behoves us to delight in the Lord and set our

affection on things above, that our motives may be pure and our desires may be holy. Such desires will surely culminate in a harvest of righteousness, peace and joy in the Holy Spirit.

The Reward of a Pure Heart

'Who may ascend into the hill of the LORD,' asked David, and *'who may stand in His holy place?'*

> *'He who has clean hands and a pure heart, who has not lifted up his soul to an idol, nor sworn deceitfully. He shall receive blessing from the LORD, and righteousness from the God of his salvation. This is Jacob, the genera-tion of those who seek Him, who seek Your face.'*
>
> (Psalm 24:4–6)

To 'lift up one's soul to an idol' is to set one's affection on and put one's trust in something other than the Lord. In Psalm 25:1, David disassociates himself from idols and those who worship them by declaring: *'To You, O LORD, I lift up my soul. O my God, I trust in You.'* Once again, the issue is loyalty or wholeness of heart. No one can serve two masters, no one can trust in two sources, and no one can delight in two lovers.

The Apostle Paul challenged the Corinthians on this very point: *'You cannot drink the cup of the Lord and the cup of demons; You cannot partake of the Lord's table and of the table of demons. Or do we provoke the Lord to jealousy? Are we stronger than He?'* (1 Corinthians 10:21–22).

The pure in heart will receive a blessing from the Lord and a bill of righteousness from the God of salvation. This 'righteousness' is a declaration of 'right-standing' with God which enables us to come into His Presence without a sense of guilt and unworthiness or fear of condemnation. Thus, the 'blessing' that God bestows upon the pure in heart is the right to ascend into the hill of the Lord and stand in His holy place.

An understanding of the Hebrew language will enhance our appreciation of this truth. There are two Hebrew words in this passage, both of which are translated as 'seek'. The first word *'darash'*, means 'to follow in pursuit' or 'to search for a desired object'. It connotes 'persistence in prayer' and 'diligence in worship'.

The second word *'baqash'*, means 'to diligently look for, to search earnestly until the object of the search is located'. It is a search that is guaranteed to succeed. Remember that the Lord said through the prophet Jeremiah, *'You will seek Me and find Me, when you search for me with all your heart'* (Jeremiah 29:13).

'Paneh', translated 'face', signifies 'God's personal and manifest Presence'. Thus, the promise of Scripture to the pure in heart is that they will not only have access to God's holy place, but will also have the privilege of offering up sacrifices of prayer and worship before His Throne, and in so doing, 'search for' and 'find' the Lord – that is, gaze upon His Glory, revel in His love, exult in His Presence, and delight in His holiness.

'They shall not come near Me'

Why is it that some people find it difficult to worship God, and try as they may, can't seem to break through into the realm of revelation and glory? A likely answer is found in the forty-fourth chapter of Ezekiel. The Lord said to the prophet, *'Mark well who may enter the house and all who go out from the sanctuary.'* **Mark well!**

> *'Thus says the LORD God: "No foreigner, uncircumcised in heart and uncircumcised in flesh, shall enter My sanctuary, including any foreigner who is among the children of Israel. And the Levites who went far from Me, when Israel went astray, who strayed away from Me after their idols, they shall bear their iniquity. Yet they shall be ministers in My sanctuary, as gatekeepers of the house and ministers of the house; they shall slay*

*the burnt offering and the sacrifice for the people, and
they shall stand before them to minister to them ... And
they shall not come near Me to minister to Me as priest,
nor come near any of My holy things, nor into the Most
Holy Place; but they shall bear their shame and their
abominations which they have committed."'*

(Ezekiel 44:9–11, 13)

Idolatry. Filthiness of the flesh and spirit. Lust of the
world. Self-centredness. Love of money. Any and all of
these sins will keep us from entering into true spiritual
worship, and hence, from experiencing God's manifest
Presence.

The Apostle James puts it this way: *'God resists the
proud, but gives grace to the humble.'* The proud are essentially 'self-worshippers' and hence, idolaters at heart. On
the other hand, purity of heart or whole-hearted love of the
Father qualifies one to enter into the Presence of God and
positions one to receive a revelation of His Glory.

The Sermon on the Mount – our Lord's classic teaching
on the Kingdom of God – is a remarkable biographical
sketch of Kingdom citizens. It defines the character and
charts the conduct of those who name the name of
Messiah. Central to the Lord's discourse is this statement:

'Blessed are the pure in heart, for they shall see God.'

(Matthew 5:8)

The Greek word *'katharos'*, translated 'pure', denotes
'that which is clean, free from impure admixture, without
blemish, undefiled'. The 'heart' is the seat of human
thought, desire and motive. The Expositor's Greek Testament makes the following observation:

'The pure may be the spotless or faultless in general;
the continent with special reference to sexual indul-
gence – those whose very thoughts are clean; or the
pure in motive, the single-minded, the men who seek

the Kingdom as the *summum bonum* with undivided heart.'

Jesus lived what He preached – the ultimate example of whole-hearted love for the Father and selfless dedication to the purposes of the Kingdom. Consider His testimony:

'I do not seek My own will but the will of the Father who sent Me ... I have come in My Father's Name ... the Living Father sent Me and I live because of the Father ... He who seeks the glory of the One who sent Him is true, and no unrighteousness is in Him ... I do nothing of Myself, but as My Father taught Me, I speak these things ... I honour My Father ... I do not seek My own glory ... Father, glorify Your Name ... That the world may know that I love the Father, and as the Father gave Me commandment, so I do.'

One can see, from the above quoted verses of John's Gospel, that Jesus was a totally 'Father-centred' Son. What was the effect of Messiah's 'Father-centredness' and purity of heart?

'For the Father loves the Son, and shows Him all things that He Himself does; and He will show Him greater works than these, that you may marvel.... And He who sent Me is with Me. The Father has not left Me alone, for I always do those things that please Him.'

(John 5:20; 8:29)

The reward of a pure heart is a manifestation of God's Presence (**the Father is with me**) and a revelation of His Glory (**the Father shows me**).

Blessed are the pure in heart for they shall see God! The Greek word *'optomai'*, translated 'see', means 'to gaze with wide open eyes as at something remarkable', and by implication, 'to discern clearly or perceive'. Hebraistically, 'to see' is 'to experience'.

The promise to the pure in heart is that they will gaze upon the glory and splendour of the Lord with wide open eyes, that is, with clear and uninhibited vision. They will come to know and understand the nature and power of the One who has called them, and in so doing, taste and see that the Lord is good. They will experience His Presence, partake of His Divine Nature, and be filled with His Holy Spirit!

The Apostle Paul highlighted the correlation between a pure heart and an open heaven in his epistle to the Church at Ephesus. They Spirit of wisdom and revelation in the knowledge of God (Ephesians 1:17) is predicated on genuine faith in the Lord Jesus and sincere love of the brethren (Ephesians 1:15).

May God grant us the privilege of being numbered among those who *'call on the Lord out of a pure heart'* and *'behold His Glory with unveiled face.'*

Chapter 6

Blessed Are They Who Hunger and Thirst

The *Shema*, the greatest commandment of all, enjoins us to *'love the Lord our God with all our heart, soul, mind and strength'* (Deuteronomy 6:5).

King David, the passionate psalmist of Israel, lived the *Shema* almost every day of his life. He was a man after God's heart, or to put it another way, 'a man after God.' Reading the Psalms, one can sense the heartcry of a man, who, because of his deep love for the Lord, was hot on God's trail. And by following that trail of ever deepening love, we too can discover the way into God's Presence.

Delighting in God

'Delight yourself also in the LORD, and He shall give you the desires of your heart' (Psalm 37:4). To delight in the Lord is to esteem the Person and Work of Messiah Jesus as life's greatest joy and most precious possession. It is 'first love' – loving Jesus first, before anything or anyone else.

> *'Yes, the Almighty will be your gold and your precious silver; for then you will have your delight in the Almighty, and lift up your face to God.'* (Job 22:25–26)

83

'Delighting in the Lord' connotes a certain abandonment of self in favour of God's will and pleasure ... covenant love in which we die to ourselves and live solely for the Lord ... an attitude of heart that declares, 'Pleasing you, pleases me.'

> *'If you turn away your foot from the Sabbath, from doing your pleasure on My holy day, and call the Sabbath a delight, the holy day of the LORD honourable, and shall honour Him, not doing your own ways, nor finding your own pleasure, nor speaking your own words, then you shall delight yourself in the LORD; and I will cause you to ride on the high hills of the earth, and feed you with the heritage of Jacob your father. The mouth of the LORD has spoken.'*   (Isaiah 58:13–14)

'Delighting in the Lord' bespeaks holy desire and spiritual hunger. The Psalmist used the analogy of a deer searching for water in the wilderness to illustrate his own hunger for the Presence of God:

> *'As the deer pants for the water brooks, so pants my soul for You, O God. My soul thirst for God, for the living God. When shall I come and appear before God?'*
>   (Psalm 42:1, 2)

Water is not an optional luxury, but a vital necessity, and all the more so in the wilderness of Judea! Indeed, water is the single most important source of nourishment and sustenance. Without it, one cannot exist for any length of time. Finding water in the wilderness, therefore, is a matter of life or death.

Thus, the Psalmist declares the Presence of God to be the most valuable commodity and fundamental necessity of life! *'I would have lost heart,'* said David, *'unless I had believed to see the goodness of the Lord in the land of the living'* (Psalm 27:13). If you have truly tasted and seen that the Lord is good, you will not be able to live without the intimacy of His Presence.

> *'O God, You are my God; early will I seek You; my soul thirsts for You; my flesh longs for you in a dry and thirsty land where there is no water. So I have looked for You in the sanctuary, to see Your power and Your glory. Because Your lovingkindness is better than life, my lips shall praise You. Thus I will bless You while I live; I will lift up my hands in Your name. My soul shall be satisfied as with marrow and fatness, and my mouth shall praise You with joyful lips. When I remember You on my bed, I meditate on You in the night watches. Because You have been my help, therefore in the shadow of Your wings I will rejoice. My soul follows close behind You; Your right hand upholds me.'* (Psalm 63:1–8)

The dry and thirsty land in which we live – this sick and sinful world – should accentuate our hunger and thirst for the purity of God's Presence and the splendour of His holiness. The corruption that is in the world through lust should drive us into the sanctuary – the pressures of the world should spur us to gather together as God's people – with an even greater desire to see God's power and glory manifested in our midst.

David comes to the realization that God's lovingkindness is better than life itself, and that the Presence of God satisfies his soul as with marrow and fatness (literally with the richest, finest and choicest part, and with abundance), and for this reason, he rejoices in the shadow of God's wings. But spiritual hunger and thirst – longing for the Presence of God – must be translated into decisive action. David says, *'Early will I seek You ... I look for You ... my lips shall praise You ... I lift up My hands in Your Name ... I meditate on You ... my soul follows close behind You.'*

The Hebrew word *'shachar'*, translated 'early', literally means 'to dawn', and figuratively, 'to rise early and to earnestly engage in a task', and by extension, 'to painstakingly search for an object'. In Psalm 130:6, a soul who waits upon God is likened to a watchman who stands on the rampart and scans the horizon for the first sign of daybreak, so that he may blow the shofar and awaken the city.

The Hebrew word *'dabaq'*, translated 'follow close', means 'to cleave, cling, join or adhere', and figuratively, 'to overtake or catch by pursuit'. Desire for God must be converted into an active seeking of Him – a veritable over-taking of and clinging to Him in prayer and worship – whether as individuals in the 'prayer-closet' or as congregations in the corporate assembly.

> *'One thing I have desired of the* Lord, *that will I seek: that I may dwell in the house of the* Lord *all the days of my life, to behold the beauty of the* Lord, *and to inquire in His temple.'*   (Psalm 27:4)

Like Martha, we are often worried about many things and try to run in seven directions at once, but only one thing is really necessary – to sit at Jesus' feet and listen to His Word. The one thing we should desire above all else is to be where God is, dwelling in His Presence, feasting at His table, surrounded by His Glory.

The Hebrew word *'yashab'*, translated 'dwell', denotes 'permanent residency', in contrast to occasional visitation. It literally means 'to sit down', and hence, 'to remain'. It is also used of 'marriage', thus signifying 'a life-long commit-ment'. As new creatures in Messiah Jesus and members of God's eternal household, it is our privilege to live each day in the power of God's Spirit and the glory of His Presence.

In His Presence one can 'dig for answers' to life's most probing questions. The Hebrew word *'baqar'*, translated 'inquire', literally means 'to plough', and figuratively, 'to search for, seek out, inspect and consider'. In His Presence one discovers the 'path of life' that leads to fullness of joy and pleasures forevermore (Psalm 16:11). It is in the Presence of Him who is the *Logos* – the sum total of Divine wisdom and knowledge – that one discovers the way, comes to know the truth, and experiences the life of God.

The priority of God's Presence is nowhere more clearly delineated than in David's anguished prayer of repentance in Psalm 51:

> *'Create in me a clean heart, O God, and renew a stead-fast spirit within me. Do not cast me away from Your Presence, and do not take Your Holy Spirit from me. Restore to me the joy of Your salvation, and uphold me by Your generous Spirit.'* (Psalm 51:10–12)

Can't you sense the cry of David's heart? 'God, whatever you do, don't exclude me from Your Presence; don't remove Your anointing from my life. Kill me, if You will, but don't let me go on living without the intimacy of Your Spirit and the knowledge of Your Glory.'

God's Presence, At All Cost

There is something about spiritual hunger that commands the attention and attracts the favour of the Lord. To an eager audience on a hillside in Galilee, Jesus said: *'Blessed are those who hunger and thirst for righteousness, for they shall be filled'* (Matthew 5:6). Implicit in this statement is an element of sanctified desperation. This is no casual enquiry or whimsical fancy, but rather, a resolute determin-ation arising from an insatiable appetite.

Moses epitomized this hunger and thirst for righteous-ness when he cried: *'If Your Presence does not go with us, do not bring us up from here!'* (Exodus 33:15). And waxing bolder, he prayed, *'Please, show me Your glory.'* The Lord's response is most instructive for modern-day seekers of righteousness:

> *'Then He said, "I will make all My goodness pass before you, and I will proclaim the Name of the LORD before you. I will be gracious to whom I will be*

gracious, and I will have compassion on whom I will have compassion."' (Exodus 33:19)

The Glory of God is the sum total of the Divine attributes – the fullness of the Divine Nature. The Glory of God bespeaks love and mercy; holiness and majesty; power and authority; wisdom and knowledge; righteousness and justice; faithfulness and immutability. Hence, the Lord's answer: *'I will make all My **goodness** pass before You, and I will proclaim the **name** of the Lord.'*

The Name of the Lord is representative of His character and attributes. The eight redemptive names by which God revealed Himself to Israel constitute eight distinctive revelations of His Divine nature and power.

However, there were tests to pass and conditions to meet before Moses could experience the answer to his prayer.

> *'And the LORD said to Moses, "Cut two tablets of stone like the first ones, and I will write on these tablets the words that were on the first tablets which you broke. So be ready in the morning, and come up in the morning to Mount Sinai, and present yourself to Me there on the top of the mountain. And no man shall come up with you, and let no man be seen throughout all the mountain; let neither flocks nor herds feed before that mountain."'*
> (Exodus 34:1–3)

'Cut two tablets of stone,' said the Lord, *'and I will write on them My laws.'* God declared through the prophet Jeremiah that in the time of the New Covenant He would put His law in people's minds and write it on their hearts (Jeremiah 31:33). We are to come before the Lord with the 'tablet' of a hungry heart and an open mind, that the Lord may write with His hand upon us all the details of His plans (1 Chronicles 28:19).

'Be ready in the morning, and come up and present yourself there on the top of the mountain.' There is a price to God's

Presence. There is a cost to knowing God and seeing His Glory. It is called *'seeking first the Kingdom.'* It is called *'denying oneself, taking up one's cross, and following Jesus.'* It is called *'losing one's life for the sake of Jesus and the Gospel.'* If we are earnest in our quest to know God, then *'whatever He says to us, we will do'* (John 2:5), even to the point of waiting in solitudinous prayer and worship until God reveals Himself.

'Present yourself' connotes the introduction of a subject to the King, or a servant to the Master, or a subordinate to the Commanding Officer. With what humility it behoves us to approach God! The how, when and where of God's revelation is His prerogative. Ours is to be in the appointed place of prayer, watching and waiting.

> *'Now the* LORD *descended in the cloud and stood with him there, and proclaimed the name of the* LORD *... So Moses made haste and bowed his head toward the earth, and worshipped. Then he said, "If now I have found grace in Your sight, O Lord, let my Lord, I pray, go among us, even though we are a stiff-necked people; and pardon our iniquity and our sin, and take us as Your inheritance." And He said, "Behold, I make a covenant. Before all your people I will do marvels such as have not been done in all the earth, nor in any nation; and all the people among whom you are shall see the work of the* LORD. *For it is an awesome thing that I will do with you."'*
> (Exodus 34:5, 8–10)

Those who desire a double portion of God's Spirit seek a hard thing. Hard, but not impossible. Hard, for it is extremely costly in terms of faith and obedience, but gloriously possible, for it is the Father's good pleasure to give us the Kingdom!

The challenge sounds forth to us today, as it did to Elisha of old: *'If you see me when I am taken from you, it shall be so for you; but if not, it shall not be so'* (2 Kings 2:10). *'If you see Me'* – if you keep seeking Jesus with a single eye; if you keep other desires from entering your heart and other objects from capturing your attention – *'then it shall be so for you!'*

God's promise stands sure: *'Those who hunger and thirst after righteousness shall be filled.'* The desperate leader cries out: 'O Lord, we acknowledge our sin, our pride, our stubbornness, and indeed, we are not worthy of Your Presence, but by Your grace, **go among us**. Take us as Your inheritance. Make us Your dwelling place. Reveal Your Glory. Pour out Your Holy Spirit.'

A cry for God's Presence that is born out of deep desire and desperate need will invariably provoke a positive response: *'I will do marvels among you. I will do an awesome thing with you. You shall see the work of the Lord in your midst!'* It is simply a question of 'plugging into' God's will!

Abide With Us

Each and every encounter **with** God, and revelation **of** God, is initiated **by** God. The Lord will call to us, as He did to Samuel, but whether or not there is an ensuing revelation of His Divine Nature and eternal purpose is largely determined by our response. *'Speak Lord, Your servant is listening,'* and other such expressions of spiritual hunger, guarantee receipt of all that God has to give.

God gives us a taste of His Presence and Glory to whet our spiritual appetite, in order to stimulate us to seek Him for even greater revelation. The admonition to *'taste and see that the Lord is good,'* climaxes with the statement that *'those who seek the Lord shall not lack any good thing'* (Psalm 34:8–10).

God will attract our attention, as He did Moses', with a manifestation of His power and glory, but whether or not we receive the full revelation of His character and redemptive purpose depends on our *'turning aside to look'* (Exodus 3:1–15). Sadly, many people are satisfied with a taste, a glimpse, a promise, and a touch. But God wants to take us deeper.

> *'Now behold, two of them were travelling that same day to a village called Emmaus, which was seven miles from Jerusalem. And they talked together of all these things which had happened. So it was, while they conversed and reasoned, that Jesus Himself drew near and went with them. But their eyes were restrained, so that they did not know Him.'*　　　　　　　　　　(Luke 24:13–16)

Often, during times of personal prayer or corporate worship, Jesus will draw near to us, as He did to the disciples on the road to Emmaus. Sometimes, in our preoccupation with other things, we are oblivious to His Presence. At other times we can sense His Presence, but our eyes are restrained, and we cannot see His purpose or understand His ways.

> *'Then they drew near to the village where they were going, and He indicated that He would have gone farther. But they constrained Him, saying, "Abide with us, for it is toward evening, and the day is far spent." And He went in to stay with them. Now it came to pass as He sat at the table with them, that He took bread, blessed and broke it, and gave it to them. Then their eyes were opened and they knew Him; and He vanished from their sight.'*　　　　　　　　　　(Luke 24:28–31)

The Lord will often give us a taste of His Presence and then act as if He is going to leave. His overwhelming desire is to stay with us and reveal Himself to us, but He will only do that if we invite Him, or more literally, **constrain** Him.

The Lord looks for a response of faith, an expression of spiritual hunger, some manifestation of holy desire. He stands at the door and knocks. If we will only open the door and entreat Him to come in, He will abide with us and reveal Himself to us in the breaking of bread – the intimate communion of covenant relationship.

Let Us Know, Let Us Pursue

The prophecy of Hosea, which essentially is a call to holiness, fidelity and intimacy with God, reveals the importance of translating Spirit-inspired desire into Spirit-led action:

> *'Let us know, let us pursue the knowledge of the LORD. His going forth is established as the morning; He will come to us like the rain, like the latter and former rain to the earth.'* (Hosea 6:3)

'Let us know the Lord.' That's the goal. To know the Lord in the intimacy of shared love. To perceive His character and understand His ways, and in so doing, to become like Him in thought (attitude), word (speech) and deed (behaviour).

Desire is one thing, but achievement is another. To know the Lord, we must pursue Him with all our being. The Hebrew word *'radaph'*, translated 'pursue', is used in some cases to denote 'persecution'. Thus, it bespeaks great intensity of purpose – singleminded devotion to a cause and relentless determination in pursuit of a goal.

The Apostle Paul described his pursuit of the knowledge of God in the Epistle to the Philippians:

> *'Yet indeed I also count all things loss for the excellence of the knowledge of Christ Jesus my Lord, for whom I have suffered the loss of all things, and count them as rubbish, that I may gain Christ and be found in Him ... that I may know Him ... Not that I have already attained, or am already perfected; but I press on, that I may lay hold of that for which Christ Jesus has also laid hold of me ... one thing I do, forgetting those things which are behind and reaching forward to those things which are ahead, I press toward the goal for the prize of the upward call of God in Christ Jesus.'* (Philippians 3:8–14)

First of all, Paul had to come to grips with the exclusivity of Messiah. *'Who is like You, O Lord, among the gods? Who is like You, glorious in holiness, fearful in praises, doing wonders?'* (Exodus 15:11). The transcendent glory of Messiah's nature and the surpassing greatness of His power demanded a casting aside of past achievements and future ambitions, in order that Paul might devote his entire energy to knowing Messiah.

Fellowship with Messiah in the fullness of His death, burial and resurrection, is riches indeed. It is *'huperecho'* (the Greek word for excellence); 'superior to anything else; the surpassing thing'.

Paul used three word pictures to depict his quest for intimacy with Messiah: 'Press on,' 'Reach forward,' and 'lay hold of.' The first word *'dioko'*, translated 'press', comes from the world of foot-racing, and means 'to pursue'. The picture is of a Greek runner, sprinting down the track to the finish line. Most importantly, it does not denote the pursuit of a constantly moving object, but rather, 'advancement toward a fixed goal!' Intimacy with Messiah is, by God's grace, a sure destination and an achievable goal!

The second word *'epekteino'*, translated 'reach', also comes from the world of athletic competition and means 'to stretch forth after'. The picture is of a runner straining every muscle as he heads toward the goal, his hand stretched out ready to grasp it. *'Epekteino'* describes the runner whose 'eye outstrips and draws onward the hand, and the hand the foot' (Wuest). When our gaze is fixed on Messiah, His vision draws us on and unto Himself (Hebrews 12:1–2).

The third word *'katalambano'*, translated 'lay hold of', means 'to seize, lay hold of and overcome'. The picture is of a football player who catches hold of his opponent and pulls him to the ground. Messiah seized Paul (Saul) on the road to Damascus and claimed him as His own, and in like manner, Paul desires to lay hold of Messiah's purpose for his life and possess it in its fullness. Paul pursued Messiah with determination and vigour, and in this sense is reminiscent of Jacob who wrestled all night with the Angel of God and would not let him go until he pronounced a blessing (Genesis 32:22–30).

But perhaps the most beautiful analogy of spiritual hunger is found in the Song of Solomon, which is itself an allegorical portrait of the relationship between God and Israel, and Messiah Jesus and the Church.

> *'By night on my bed I sought the one I love; I sought him, but I did not find him. "I will rise now," I said, "And go about the city; in the streets and in the squares I will seek the one I love." I sought him, but I did not find him. The watchmen who go about the city found me; I said, "Have you seen the one I love?" Scarcely had I passed by them, when I found the one I love. I held him and would not let him go, until I had brought him to the house of my mother, and into the chamber of her who conceived me.'*
>
> (Song of Solomon 3:1–4)

Spiritual hunger is often accentuated in the night hours, when the hustle and bustle and busyness of life subsides, and one's heart and mind grows quiet before the Lord. It is in the night hours, when we are free from the distractions of life, that the Lord can most easily get our attention. It therefore behoves us to yield to spiritual hunger pains whenever they come upon us, for the longing of the heart, the awakening of desire, and the urge to pray are evidences of the moving of the Holy Spirit in our inner man.

Let us do as the Shulamite did in the Song of Songs: Get out of bed and seek the One we love, and having found Him, not let Him go until His purpose is accomplished in us. Make it your prayer today:

> *'... O LORD, we have waited for You; the desire of our soul is for Your Name and for the remembrance of You. With my soul I have desired You in the night, yes, by my spirit within me I will seek You early ...'*
>
> (Isaiah 26:8b–9a)

Chapter 7

God's Presence, God's Way

David, the man after God's heart, is in many respects an Old Testament version of the Apostle Peter. Zealous. Fervent. Audacious. And rather impetuous. But most of all, he was a man who loved God with all his heart and desired nothing more than to be in His Presence.

The quest to bring up the Ark of the Covenant from Kirjath Jearim to Jerusalem exemplified David's passion for the Presence and Glory of God. The Book of Chronicles records this as the first event of David's reign over united Israel – first, not in sequence of history but in order of priority.

> 'Then David consulted with the captains of thousands and hundreds, and with every leader. And David said to all the assembly of Israel, "If it seems good to you, and if it is of the LORD our God, let us send out to our brethren everywhere who are left in all the land of Israel, and with them to the priests and Levites who are in their cities and their common-lands, that they may gather together to us; And let us bring the ark of our God back to us, for we have not inquired at it since the days of Saul." Then all the assembly said that they would do so, for the thing was right in the eyes of all the people. So David gathered all Israel together, from Shihor in Egypt to as far as the entrance of Hamath, to bring the ark of God from Kirjath Jearim.' (1 Chronicles 13:1–5)

So far, so good! A national consensus on the need for revival. A corporate desire to restore the Ark – the very Presence and Glory of God – to its rightful place at the centre of Israeli society. However, David's experience demonstrates that it is possible to have the right desire, but the wrong attitude. And a wrong attitude always results in wrong behaviour.

> *'And David and all Israel went up to Baalah, to Kirjath Jearim, which belonged to Judah, to bring up from there the ark of God the* LORD, *who dwells between the cherubim, where His name is proclaimed. So they carried the ark of God on a new cart from the house of Abinadab, and Uzza and Ahio drove the cart. Then David and all Israel played music before God with all their might, with singing, on harps, on stringed instruments, on tambourines, on cymbals, and with trumpets. And when they came to Chidon's threshing floor, Uzza put out his hand to hold the ark, for the oxen stumbled. Then the anger of the* LORD *was aroused against Uzza, and He struck him because he put his hand to the ark; and he died there before God.'* (1 Chronicles 13:6–10)

God's instruction to Moses was clear: *'You shall make poles of acacia wood, and overlay them with gold. You shall put the poles into the rings on the sides of the ark, that the ark may be carried by them'* (Exodus 25:13, 14). And moreover, *'When the camp is set to go, then the sons of Kohath shall come to carry them; but they shall not touch any holy thing, lest they die'* (Numbers 4:15).

The Ark of the Covenant was to be carried on the shoulders of the priests in the manner prescribed by Moses, not transported on a man-made, oxen-driven cart. The Presence of God is borne by people, not things. God dwells in spiritual temples made of living stones, not in temples made with hands. Neither can He be worshipped in an acceptable way with the creation of men's hands (Acts 17:24–25).

Granted, it was a new cart and probably the best one they could find, but even man's best is not good enough for God. Man's good works are, at best, 'dead' or spiritually unfruitful. Indeed, the wisdom of this world is foolishness in the sight of the Lord (1 Corinthians 1:20). Human flesh has nothing whatever to boast of in God's Presence.

Once before, the Ark of the Covenant had been transported on a new cart when it was returned to the people of Israel by the disease-stricken Philistines. The Philistines acted on the limited amount of spiritual knowledge they possessed, and God honoured their efforts. But for David and the people of Israel, it was an altogether different matter.

They had the Word of God, but failed to take it seriously. They had the knowledge of God's ways, as recorded by His servant Moses, but preferred to embrace the world's way of doing things. They tried to do God's work, the world's way. To apply the world's methods to God's ministry.

But it didn't work then, and it won't work now. The natural man does not receive the things of the Spirit of God, and natural methods do not produce spiritual results.

The Rock Music Cart

A modern counterpart to David's new cart is 'Christian rock music'. The very name, 'Christian Rock', is a misnomer, for the two words are antithetical terms, representing two conflicting spirits, two opposing kingdoms, and two variant ways of life. People think that by playing the world's music they will attract young people to the church, and indeed they do. But rock 'n' roll music will not change people's lives, nor will it summon the Presence of God.

On one occasion I had a vision of a Christian Youth Rally. The Lord Jesus was standing in the centre of the hall, and every one of the thousands of young people passed before Him. As I watched the vision, it seemed that to over half of the supposedly 'Christian' young people, Jesus said, *'Depart from Me, I do not know You.'*

The implication of the vision is clear: It is not enough to attract young people to youth rallies or church meetings, albeit through 'user-friendly' mediums. They must have a life-changing encounter with the Living Messiah, or else they will remain lost.

There was a certain arrogance and presumption in David's decision to transport the Ark on a new cart. It was as if he was saying to God, 'Lord, I know what You said to Moses, but times have changed. We're living in a new day, with new technology and new value systems.' David was not just disobeying God, he was actually supplanting God. In reality, he was saying, 'God, I know more than You do; my way is better than Your way.' And that, surely, is the ultimate expression of pride.

It is the same in the Church today. The Bible clearly says, *'Do not be conformed to this world'* (Romans 12:2). That means in dress, in conduct, in attitude, in method, in music, in every way. One can either have the spirit of the world or the Spirit who is from God, but not a mixture of both. Yet we dress like the world, play music like the world and entertain like the world, believing that it will make us relevant and acceptable to the world.

The most relevant church in society is a Christ-like Church ... a Church that holds fast to the standard of God's Word ... a Church that is filled with the power of the Holy Spirit ... a Church that shines as a light in the midst of spiritual darkness ... a Church that is in the world but not of it.

It Takes More Than Praise

The charismatic movement emphasized praise to the point of extremism and imbalance. Praise is a wonderful truth and an important part of the Christian life, but it takes more than praise to bring us into the Presence of God.

The same man who stated that *'God inhabits the praises of His people,'* also declared, *'Who may ascend into the hill of the Lord, or who may stand in His holy place? He who has clean hands and a pure heart...* ' (Psalm 24:3–4). A pure heart has to do with attitude, and clean hands have to do with obedience, or doing things God's way.

In our case study, David and all Israel played music before the Lord with all their might. If praise is all that is required to usher one into the Presence of God, then these celebrating Hebrews should have had a 'glory time'. But as we have noted, David's attitude toward God was wrong – his heart was not altogether pure – and his actions reflected his attitude – his hands were not completely clean.

Thus, in the midst of a dynamic praise session, judgment fell! The oxen stumbled, Uzza stretched out his hand to steady the Ark, God's anger was aroused, and He struck Uzza dead! Mark well: if we don't do it God's way, something is bound to go wrong.

I often wonder what kind of judgment will befall the Church as a result of its flirting with the world's methodology. The Christian music scene, for example, is littered with the casualties of Divine judgment on a hybrid system. One thing is for sure: Jesus is coming into the temple of God to drive out all those who 'buy and sell' and to overturn the tables of the 'money changers' – those who prostitute the ministry of God for commercial profit and who introduce the ways of the world into the House of the Lord. In the end, every vessel in Jerusalem and Judah shall be holy to the Lord, and there shall not be any 'Canaanites' (greedy, unclean merchants) in the House of the Lord (Zechariah 14:21)

Uzza's impetuosity and irreverence cost him his life, but it was David who made the biggest mistake of all. If, according to his own admission, they had 'consulted God about the proper order,' and had humbled themselves to walk in God's way, the Ark would not have threatened to overturn and Uzza would not have had occasion to steady it.

Interestingly enough, David's first reaction was to blame God for His perceived harshness, rather than to accept responsibility for not walking in God's ways:

> *'And David became angry because of the LORD's outbreak against Uzza; therefore that place is called Perez Uzza to this day. David was afraid of God that day, saying, "How can I bring the ark of God to me?" So David would not move the ark with him into the City of David, but took it aside into the house of Obed-Edom the Gittite. The ark of God remained with the family of Obed-Edom in his house three months. And the LORD blessed the house of Obed-Edom and all that he had.'*
>
> (1 Chronicles 13:11–14)

However, during the ensuing three months God apparently dealt with David's heart attitude and freshly imparted to him a spirit of humility in the fear of the Lord. David acknowledged his error and embraced the way of the Lord, as set down in His Word.

> *'Then David said, "No one may carry the ark of God but the Levites, for the LORD has chosen them to carry the ark of God and to minister before Him forever." ... And David called for Zadok and Abiathar the priests, and for the Levites: for Uriel, Asaiah, Joel, Shemaiah, Eliel, and Amminadab. He said to them, "You are the heads of the fathers' houses of the Levites; sanctify yourselves, you and your brethren, that you may bring up the ark of the LORD God of Israel to the place I have prepared for it. For because you did not do it the first time, the LORD our God broke out against us, because we did not consult Him about the proper order." ... And the children of the Levites bore the ark of God on their shoulders, by its poles, as Moses had commanded according to the word of the LORD.'*
>
> (1 Chronicles 15:2, 11–13, 15)

This time everything was different. Because David walked in God's way there was a release of joy among the people as they brought up the Ark, and the blessing of the Lord enabled them to successfully complete the mission.

I cannot overstate the importance of walking in God's ways. Simply desiring God's Presence is not enough. If we are to see the full manifestation of His Glory, we must walk in His ways. Those who worship Him must worship in spirit and in truth.

The Old Testament concept of walking in God's ways is realized in the New Testament concept of discipleship. Jesus came, not just to seek and save the lost, but to make disciples. Discipleship is the purpose of salvation.

Simply defined, a disciple is a committed follower of the Lord – that is, one who lives under the discipline of Messiah, who takes His Word seriously and obeys it implicitly, and who walks in God's ways rather than his own. Jesus taught that discipleship is the key to knowing and experiencing God:

> *'He who has My commandments and keeps them, it is he who loves Me. And he who loves Me will be loved by My Father, and I will love him and manifest Myself to him. . . . If anyone loves Me, he will keep My word; and My Father will love him, and We will come to him and make Our home with him.'* (John 14:21, 23)

Commitment, issuing in obedience, is the ultimate evidence of genuine love. Jesus says, 'I love the one who loves Me and demonstrates it by leading a life of obedience; such a one will receive a special blessing – I will manifest Myself to him.' The Greek word *'emphanidzo'*, translated 'manifest', is derived from *'phaino'*, 'to cause to shine'. Thus, it means 'to appear, come to view, reveal, exhibit, make visible, present oneself in the sight of another, be conspicuous'.

The reward of a disciple is nothing less than a personal visitation of the Lord and a supernatural revelation of His Glory. Once again, it is a case of 'God's Presence, God's Way.' There is no shortcut to the abiding Presence of the Lord.

101

In Spirit and in Truth

Worship, real spiritual worship, is not so much an action that one performs, but rather, an attitude that one holds toward God. The ancient mystics spoke of worship as a poise of heart or a disposition of soul. In the final analysis, worship is being in the Presence of God and loving Him ... adoring Him ... glorifying Him ... for Who He is and what He has done! There is no better picture of worship than that of the twenty-four elders in the Book of Revelation, falling down before the One who sits on the Throne.

> *'The four living creatures, each having six wings, were full of eyes around and within. And they do not rest day or night, saying: "Holy, holy, holy, Lord God Almighty, Who was and is and is to come!" Whenever the living creatures give glory and honour and thanks to Him who sits on the throne, who lives forever and ever, the twenty-four elders fall down before Him who sits on the throne and worship Him who lives forever and ever, and cast their crowns before the throne, saying: "You are worthy, O Lord, to receive glory and honour and power; for You created all things, and by Your will they exist and were created."'* (Revelation 4:8–11)

The act of falling down is a symbol of selfless abandonment, a total pouring out of one's being in deference to the honour and glory of God. Furthermore, the elders took their crowns and **cast them** before the Throne. Worship is the taking of all that God has given us – gifts and callings, enduements of power and delegations of authority – and returning it to Him. Laying it all before His greater glory and honour and power and authority.

The place of worship is also a place of revelation wherein one perceives the true nature and character of God. Worship is recognizing God's 'worthship' – crying out in adoration, 'Holy, holy, holy ... You are worthy O Lord!'

The biblical concept of worship presupposes a manifestation of God's Presence. True worship, therefore, is synonymous with the Presence of God. For this reason, it is patently absurd to talk of 'worshipping from afar.'

Jesus spoke about entering into God's Presence – the path of true spiritual worship – in His discourse with the woman at Jacob's well. The only acceptable kind of worship, and the only kind of worship that will lead one into the Presence of God, is worship 'in spirit and truth.'

Worship involves the soul and body, but essentially concerns the heart. It flows from one's innermost being like rivers of water. It is the natural and spontaneous response of the human heart to the revealed Glory of God. As such, it cannot be feigned or replicated. It must be fresh and new every day.

Likewise, worship must be 'in truth.' The Greek word *'aletheia'*, translated 'truth', signifies 'the reality lying at the basis of an appearance; the manifested, veritable essence of a matter' (Cremer). It denotes 'veracity, reality, sincerity, accuracy, integrity, truthfulness, dependability and propriety'. It is the opposite of that which is fictitious, feigned or false. Moreover, to worship 'in truth' is 'to have a truthful conception of the One whom we worship'. It must correspond with reality, both in regard to the object and the manner of worship.

God has a 'reality gauge' with which He measures the worship of His people. Thus, the humble imploration of a convicted publican, *'God be merciful to me a sinner,'* is more acceptable in the Lord's sight than the eloquent prayer of a self-righteous Pharisee! (Luke 18:10–14).

The worship that enters into the Presence of God is sincere and without admixture. It is not worked up or shouted down. It is real – a real response to a real revelation of a real God!

Offering Profane Fire

The danger of approaching God with wrong attitudes and

impure motives was twice demonstrated during Israel's odyssey through the wilderness.

> *'Then Nadab and Abihu, the sons of Aaron, each took his censer and put fire in it, put incense on it, and offered profane fire before the LORD, which He had not commanded them. So fire went out from the LORD and devoured them, and they died before the LORD. And Moses said to Aaron, "This is what the LORD spoke, saying: 'By those who come near Me I must be regarded as holy; and before all the people I must be glorified.' " So Aaron held his peace.'* (Leviticus 10:1–3)

The act of offering profane fire before the Lord reflected a deep-seated attitude of irreverence and contempt for the holiness of God. Approaching God anyway we please, doing our own thing in His Presence, worshipping the way we want, is profanity – an affront to His holiness. And such impertinence will surely be judged.

The Church at Corinth experienced the same kind of problem in their corporate worship. People were eating and drinking at the Lord's Table in an unworthy manner, disrespectfully and flirtatiously, not attributing the full worth of Messiah's redeeming work to the action they were performing. Their failure to 'discern the Lord's body' – that is, to carefully evaluate and properly appreciate His sacrifice – brought judgment upon themselves in the form of weakness, sickness and premature death (see 1 Corinthians 10 and 11).

The second example of profane worship is found in Numbers chapter sixteen, in the rebellion of Korah, Dathan and Abiram.

> *'Now Korah the son Izhar, the son of Kohath, the son of Levi, with Dathan and Abiram the sons of Eliab, and On the son of Peleth, sons of Reuben, took men; and they rose up before Moses with some of the children of Israel, two hundred and fifty leaders of the congregation,*

> *representatives of the congregation, men of renown.*
> *They gathered together against Moses and Aaron, and*
> *said to them, "You take too much upon yourselves, for*
> *all the congregation is holy, every one of them, and the*
> *LORD is among them. Why then do you exalt yourselves*
> *above the assembly of the LORD?"'* (Numbers 16:1–3)

The attitudes and motives of these insurrectionists is
plain to see: pride, rebellion, resentment, envy, and selfish
ambition. But Moses wisely put the matter in perspective
when he said, *'Tomorrow morning the Lord will show who is*
His and who is set aside for His use, and will cause him to
come near to Him. That one whom He chooses He will cause
to come near to Him ... You take too much upon yourselves,
you sons of Levi!' Moreover, Moses instructed Korah and
his company to present themselves before the Lord on the
following day, each with a censer and an offering of incense.

> *'So every man took his censer, put fire in it, laid incense*
> *on it, and stood at the door of the tabernacle of meeting*
> *with Moses and Aaron. And Korah gathered all the*
> *congregation against them at the door of the tabernacle*
> *of meeting. Then the glory of the LORD appeared to all*
> *the congregation.'* (Numbers 16:18–19)

How foolish and dangerous to approach God in this way.
Seeking to prove something, not just to Moses and Aaron
and the rest of the people, but to God Himself. Demanding
their rights and asserting their privileges. But God resists
the proud, and my, oh my, what resistance they encountered!

> *'Now it came to pass, as he finished speaking all these*
> *words, that the ground split apart under them, and the*
> *earth opened its mouth and swallowed them up, with*
> *their households and all the men with Korah, with all*
> *their goods. So they and all those with them went down*
> *alive into the pit; the earth closed over them, and they*

perished from among the assembly ... and a fire came out from the LORD and consumed the two hundred and fifty men who were offering incense.'

(Numbers 16:31–33, 35)

If our worship is to be acceptable to God, it must be offered as a sacrifice. The word 'sacrifice' connotes humility and gratitude – the very opposite to the spirit of Korah! The Apostle Paul urged believers *'to present their bodies to God as living sacrifices, holy and acceptable to Him,'* for such sacrificial offerings constitute a *'reasonable service of worship'* (Romans 12:1).

A New and Living Way

'Let us therefore come boldly to the throne of grace,' declared the writer to the Hebrews, *'that we may obtain mercy and find grace to help in time of need'* (Hebrews 4:16).

The word 'boldly' does not imply presumptive arrogance or brash aggression. Rather, it denotes freedom and confidence, based on the sure knowledge of Messiah's finished work and the Father's loving acceptance. Thank God, we can approach the Throne any time day or night, and be certain of a royal welcome.

However, Hebrews 4:16, as wonderful as it is, is only one half of the picture. The rest of the picture is found in Hebrews 10:19–22;

'Therefore, brethren, having boldness to enter the Holiest by the blood of Jesus, by a new and living way which He consecrated for us, through the veil, that is, His flesh, and having a High Priest over the house of God, let us draw near with a true heart in full assurance of faith, having our hearts sprinkled from an evil conscience and our bodies washed with pure water.'

There is boldness to enter the Holiest by the blood of Jesus, but we must enter in the Divinely appointed manner.

We must draw near to God with a sincere heart and with unwavering faith; with a clean conscience and a sanctified body. Then and only then will we experience the fullness of God's Presence in our lives.

Chapter 8

Building the Lord's House

The temple of Solomon is, in many respects, a prophetic type of the Church that Jesus is building among the nations. There are many principles to be gleaned and lessons to be learned from the biblical narrative by today's spiritual 'stone-cutters'. Indeed, *'all these things happened to them as examples, and were written for our instruction, upon whom the ends of the ages have come'* (1 Corinthians 10:11).

> *'So all the work that Solomon had done for the house of the LORD was finished; and Solomon brought in the things which his father David had dedicated: the silver and the gold and all the furnishings. And he put them in the treasuries of the house of God.'* (2 Chronicles 5:1)

We are called to build the House of the Lord on the foundations of former generations. The Lord says to His people, *'Stand in the ways and see, and ask for the old paths, where the good way is, and walk in it; then you will find rest for your souls'* (Jeremiah 6:16), and moreover, *'Do not remove the ancient landmark which your fathers have set'* (Proverbs 22:28). In other words, don't disdain the work of God in past generations ... the truth that was revealed, the lessons that were learned, the progress that was made. Rather, honour those who have gone before, thank God for their work, and **build on it**!

The call to honour one's father and mother is not just a requisite to respect one's immediate biological forebears, but to appreciate the pioneering generations, both natural and spiritual, which have prepared the way for us to be where we are today. The present is the child of the past. We are products of our predecessors' perseverance and heirs of their faithfulness. A man in point is Timothy, whom Paul declared to be the heir of two generations of faith (2 Timothy 1:5).

We are not called to live in the past, but to build on the past. To augment the vision, dedication and sacrifice of preceding generations. It was Solomon's building, but it was based upon David's Divinely-inspired plan, utilizing David's Divinely-supplied materials, in accordance with David's Divinely-received promises. Like Solomon, the present generation must evince an attitude of humility toward those who have gone before, if it is to realize its potential and destiny in God.

Moreover, we must see ourselves as the continuum of God's work in history. A consciousness of our heritage, and indeed, of our spiritual roots, gives us a sense of stability and security in the sovereign plan of God, and imbues us with a spirit of humility, thereby qualifying us for usefulness in the Lord's service. As the Apostle Paul wrote, *'What do you have that you did not receive?'* (1 Corinthians 4:7), and *'remember that you do not support the root, but the root supports you'* (Romans 11:18).

Solomon recognized this fact, declaring to the whole assembly of Israel at the dedication of the temple,

> *'Blessed be the LORD God of Israel, who has fulfilled with His hands what He spoke with His mouth to my father David ... So the LORD has fulfilled His word which he spoke, and I have filled the position of my father David, and sit on the throne of Israel, as the LORD promised; and I have built the temple for the name of the LORD God of Israel.'*
>
> (2 Chronicles 6:4, 10)

For this reason, I constantly urge Christians to become students of history. Don't waste your time watching television; read a history book! Examine the lives of great men and women of God. Read about past revivals. Study the restoration of the Church from the Reformation to the present day. Study the restoration of the prophetic State of Israel. Read good, accurate history books that demonstrate God's sovereignty in world affairs.

Furthermore, familiarize yourself with your personal heritage – the roots of your family, your church, the movement of which you are a part etc. I sat at the feet of my late grandfather on many occasions, listening in awe to the dramatic story of his conversion to Christ in rural Victoria, wondering at the sovereign intervention of God and the manifest destiny of our family, identifying with Grandpa as he entered the ministry of the Salvation Army, and then, upon reading *The Bridal Call*, a magazine of Aimee Semple McPherson and the Foursquare Gospel Church, audaciously visited a Pentecostal Church where he was filled with the Holy Spirit and spoke in other tongues.

All too frequently we find fault with our spiritual predecessors. Certainly they made mistakes, but then, who doesn't? May God help us dig through the rubble to find the treasures of former generations – the secrets of their success, their spiritual victories, and their knowledge of God.

In All Your Getting, Get the Presence of God

The Presence of God is the principal thing; therefore, in all our getting, we must get His manifest Presence. The House (Church) is a means to an end – a habitation for the Presence of God – and not an end in itself.

> *'Now Solomon assembled the elders of Israel and all the heads of the tribes, the chief fathers of the children of Israel, in Jerusalem, that they might bring the ark of the covenant of the LORD up from the City of David, which is*

> *Zion.... So all the elders of Israel came, and the Levites*
> *took up the ark.... Then the priests brought in the ark*
> *of the covenant of the LORD to its place, into the inner*
> *sanctuary of the temple, to the Most Holy Place...'*
>
> (2 Chronicles 5:2, 4, 7)

The Presence of God should occupy the central place of all worship and ministry, indeed, of the whole spiritual building. The Presence of God is the 'heart' of the Church, from whence life flows to every department of the congregation. If we appoint the Presence of God its rightful place in our personal and community life, just as Solomon appointed the Ark 'its place' in the Temple, we will become healthily focused on the Head of the Church (see Colossians 2:19).

The 'Ark' is the centre-piece of the 'House'. To the Church at Corinth, the Apostle Paul wrote, *'whatever you do, do all to the glory of God'* (1 Corinthians 10:31). Everything we do as 'the Church' should revolve around and issue in the manifest Presence of God.

> *'Then the priests brought in the ark of the covenant of*
> *the LORD to its place, into the inner sanctuary of the*
> *temple, to the Most Holy Place, under the wings of the*
> *cherubim. For the cherubim spread their wings over*
> *the place of the ark, and the cherubim overshadowed the*
> *ark and its poles.'* (2 Chronicles 5:7–8)

The manifest Presence of God in the Church summons the attendance of the heavenly Host. The Lord is enthroned in the corporate worship of His people, and wherever the Lord is, and wherever His Throne is established, the Heavenly Host will be assembled in splendour and majesty. *'Around the throne were four living creatures saying, "Holy, holy, holy, Lord God Almighty, Who was and is and is to come!" ... I heard the voice of many angels around the throne and the number of them was ten thousand times ten thousand, and thousands of thousands, saying with a*

112

loud voice: "Worthy is the Lamb who was slain..."'
(Revelation 4:6, 8, 5:11, 12).

The Spirit and the Word

The Ark contained two tablets of stone on which were inscribed, by the finger of God, the 'Ten Words of the covenant,' thus signifying the unanimity of the Spirit and the Word.

At the beginning of creation, the Holy Spirit is seen hovering over the face of the deep, preparing the way for the Word of God, and moving to fulfil the command as soon as it is spoken (Genesis 1:2, 3). Again, in Isaiah 59:21 the Spirit and the Word are linked in complementary union: *'As for Me,' says the LORD, 'this is My covenant with them: My Spirit who is upon you, and My words which I have put in your mouth, shall not depart from your mouth...'*

Anticipating New Covenant grace, the prophet Joel declared, *'I will pour out My Spirit on all flesh; your sons and your daughters shall prophesy...'* (Joel 2:28). And in fulfilment of his words, *'they were all filled with the Holy Spirit and began to speak with other tongues, as the Spirit gave them utterance'* (Acts 2:4).

Moreover, *'Peter, filled with the Holy Spirit, said to them...'* (Acts 4:8), and, *'they were all filled with the Holy Spirit, and they spoke the Word of God with boldness'* (Acts 4:31), and, *'when Paul had laid hands on them, the Holy Spirit came upon them, and they spoke with tongues and prophesied'* (Acts 19:6), and, *'be filled with the Spirit, speaking to one another in psalms and hymns and spiritual songs, singing and making melody in your heart to the Lord'* (Ephesians 5:18, 19).

The Spirit inspires the Word, empowers the Word, confirms the Word, and executes the Word.

> *'... the Levites who were the singers, all those of Asaph and Heman and Jeduthun, with their sons and their brethren, stood at the east end of the altar, clothed in*

white linen, having cymbals, stringed instruments and harps, and with them one hundred and twenty priests sounding with trumpets – Indeed it came to pass, when the trumpeters and singers were as one, to make one sound to be heard in praising and thanking the LORD, and when they lifted up their voice with the trumpets and cymbals and instruments of music, and praised the LORD, saying: "For He is good, for His mercy endures forever," that the house, the house of the LORD, was filled with a cloud, so that the priests could not continue ministering because of the cloud; for the glory of the LORD filled the house of God.'   (2 Chronicles 5:12–14)

Centuries later, during the Festival of *Shavuot*, the Holy Spirit was poured out on another company of 120 priests. They too were clothed in 'white linen,' which, spiritually speaking, is the righteous acts of the saints (Revelation 19:8). (In order for prayer and praise to be effectual, it must be offered in righteousness – James 5:16 and Malachi 3:3.) And they too were 'blowing trumpets,' that is, lifting up their voices to God in prayer, praise and prophetic utterance. Indeed, men from every nation under heaven heard them speaking in their native tongues the wonderful works of God (Acts 2:11).

Just as in the days of Solomon's temple, when the trumpeters and singers made one sound to be heard in praising and thanking the Lord, and the manifest Presence of God filled the house, so in the days of the Early Church, the believers lifted their voice to God with one accord in prayer and praise, and the place where they were assembled was shaken, and they were all filled with the Holy Spirit (Acts 4:24–31).

It is instructive to note the words the singers employed in praising and thanking the Lord: *'For He is good, for His mercy endures forever.'* They addressed the Glory of God in the invisible realm; they extolled the virtues and excellencies of the Divine Nature; they proclaimed the greatness of God. And as they did, that which was invisible, was made manifest. That which was hidden from the five senses of human perception, was revealed by the power of the Holy Spirit.

In prayer, praise and prophetic utterance, *'one speaks and it is done, one commands and it stands fast'* (c.p. Psalm 33:9). Under the anointing of the Holy Spirit one says, *'Let there be,'* and immediately there is (c.p. Genesis 1:3). We eat the fruit of the lips of praise (Proverbs 18:20–21) We have what we say in prayer (Mark 11:23–24).

Riding in the Vanguard

God has invested tremendous power, or, dare we say, unlimited power in the spoken word and the medium of music. *'Death and life are in the power of the tongue, and those who love it will eat its fruit'* (Proverbs 18:21). *'A word fitly spoken is like apples of gold in settings of silver'* (Proverbs 25:11). *'The tongue is a little member and boasts great things . . . the tongue is so set among our members that it defiles the whole body, and sets on fire the course of nature'* (James 3:5–6).

Thus, singers and musicians are to be a prophetic community, riding in the vanguard of the manifestation of the Spirit. As they 'prophesy on their instruments,' the Hand of the Lord comes upon the congregation and the Glory of God is revealed in people's lives in the form of salvation, deliverance, healing, encouragement, joy, peace, confirmation, guidance etc.

- When the musician played for Elisha, the Hand of the Lord (the anointing of the Holy Spirit) came upon him, and he prophesied of God's miracle-working power (2 Kings 3:15–19).
- When David played skilfully on the harp, the distressing spirit departed from Saul (albeit temporarily), and he was refreshed and made well (1 Samuel 16:23).
- When the choir of Judah led the army into battle, proclaiming, *'Praise the Lord, for His mercy endures forever,'* God's mercy was manifested in a tangible

way. The Lord set ambushes against Judah's enemies, and they were defeated (2 Chronicles 20:21–22).
- When Paul and Silas prayed and sang hymns of praise to God at midnight during their incarceration at Philippi, a great earthquake shook the foundations of the prison, and immediately all the doors were opened, and everyone's chains were loosed (Acts 16:25–26).
- When believers gather together, they are to teach and admonish one another in psalms and hymns and spiritual songs and impart grace to one another through the spoken word, and thereby build up the Body of Messiah (Colossians 3:16 and Ephesians 4:29, 5:19).

An Unhindered Flow of Blessing

In Psalm 133, the blessing of the Lord is depicted as flowing from the head to the beard and down the garments, thus covering the whole body. God intends for His blessing to flow unhindered through the leadership of the Church into the life of every member of the congregation.

The shepherd is the 'door' of the sheep (John 10:7). Thus, when Jesus, the Head of the Church, wanted to speak into the life of the seven congregations of provincial Asia, He addressed the 'messenger' or presiding elder of each congregation (see Revelation 2 and 3). Significantly, Jesus did not by-pass the men whom the Holy Spirit had appointed as overseers of the flock of God, and sneak in the back door. Like a General on a tour of inspection, He addressed the commanding officer in each region with words of commendation and/or rebuke, as the occasion demanded.

In like manner, God dealt with the congregation of Israel at the dedication of the temple and extended His blessing upon them through the wise and anointed leadership of Solomon:

> *'Then the king turned around and blessed the whole assembly of Israel, while all the assembly of Israel was standing. And he said, "Blessed be the LORD God of*

> *Israel, who has fulfilled with His hands what He spoke with His mouth to my father David, saying . . . " '*
>
> (2 Chronicles 6:3–4)

If we build the House of the Lord aright and learn, as congregations, to come into the Lord's Presence in His prescribed way, the blessing of the Lord will flow through the leadership to the whole Church. The grace of God will flow through the five-fold ministry offices, and these gifted men and women will equip the saints to do the work of ministering, which will result in a general building up of the Body of Messiah (Ephesians 4:11–12).

The two ingredients that must, of necessity, be found in leadership in order to obtain an unhindered flow of Divine blessing are **faith** and **humility**. Solomon exhibited both of these traits in his dedicatory prayer.

Firstly, Solomon *'stood before the altar of the LORD in the presence of all the assembly of Israel, and spread out his hands,'* and then *'knelt down on his knees before all the assembly of Israel and spread out his hands toward heaven.'* From this position of self-humbling, in the Presence of the Lord and in the presence of the people he was appointed to lead, Solomon called upon the Lord to keep His covenant, fulfil His promises, and bless His people, Israel.

Moreover, Solomon pressed in, by faith, to the manifest Presence of God:

> ' *"Now, my God, I pray, let Your eyes be open and let Your ears be attentive to the prayer made in this place. Now therefore, arise O LORD God, to Your resting place, You and the ark of Your strength. Let Your priests, O LORD God, be clothed with salvation, and let Your saints rejoice in goodness. O LORD God, do not turn away the face of Your Anointed; remember the mercies of Your servant David." . . . When Solomon had finished praying, fire came down from heaven and consumed the burnt offering and the sacrifices; and the glory of the LORD filled the temple. And the priests could not enter the*

house of the LORD, because the glory of the LORD had filled the LORD's house.'

(2 Chronicles 6:40–42; 7:1–2)

The spirit of dedication attracts the fire of God. Dedication that is expressed through fervent prayer, loving worship, whole-hearted obedience, and self-effacing humility.

The manifest Presence of God is an indication of Divine approval, a sign that God is well-pleased with His House. May the Almighty One find us to be such a suitable dwelling place – fit for the habitation of a King!

Chapter 9

Let God Arise!

Some people would have us believe that the devil is on a
parity with Almighty God in terms of power and authority.
The devil himself would certainly like to think that!
However, the truth is that Satan, or 'Lucifer' as he was
formerly known, is a created and finite being, and no match
whatsoever for the Creator and Sovereign Lord of the
universe.

Once and only once did Satan dare to lead an insurrec-
tion against the Throne of God, on which occasion he was
summarily cast out of Heaven and banished to the atmo-
spheric heavens surrounding the Earth. Many scholars
believe that the lamentation against the King of Tyre in
Ezekiel chapter 28 and the proverb against the King of
Babylon in Isaiah chapter 14 are descriptions of the fall
of Satan in eternity past.

> 'You were the anointed cherub who covers; I established
> you; You were on the holy mountain of God; You walked
> back and forth in the midst of fiery stones. You were
> perfect in your ways from the day you were created, till
> iniquity was found in you. By the abundance of your
> trading you became filled with violence within, and you
> sinned; therefore I cast you as a profane thing out of the
> mountain of God; and I destroyed you, O covering
> cherub, from the midst of the fiery stones.'
>
> (Ezekiel 28:14–16)

The Hebrew word *'chalal'*, translated 'profane', means 'to bore through', and by implication, 'to fatally wound, afflict, make weak or sick', and hence, 'to defile or profane'.

In contrast to his former glory, Satan was cast out of Heaven as a totally perverted being – a murderer, a thief and a liar, full of bitterness and resentment, intoxicated with pride and consumed with lust – the personification of all evil. Jesus described Satan as being *'a murderer from the beginning,'* who *'does not stand in the truth, because there is no truth in him. When he speaks a lie, he speaks from his own resources, for he is a liar and the father of it'* (John 8:44).

In other words, the very essence of Satan's being is falsehood – the perversion, and thus, the antithesis of all that is true in God's creation. He is further described in the Book of Revelation as the *'great dragon'* and the *'serpent of old,'* called *'the Devil and Satan'* who *'deceives the whole world'* (Revelation 12:9), and the *'accuser of our brethren, who accused them before our God day and night'* (Revelation 12:10). Moreover, he comes down to the earth with *'great wrath, because he knows that he has a short time'* (Revelation 12:12).

The words 'Devil' and 'Satan' are not proper names as such, but titles that depict the enemy's character and behaviour. The Greek word *'diabolos'*, translated 'devil', means 'accuser or slanderer'. 'Satan' is literally 'an adversary or opponent, one who resists, obstructs, and hinders whatever is good, a hateful enemy'.

Such was the incorrigible state of Satan upon his expulsion from Heaven, a state that exists unto the present day. The Lord, through the prophet Ezekiel, described Satan's abject humiliation and eternal disgrace: *'... I cast you to the ground, I laid you before kings, that they might gaze at you ... I brought fire from your midst; it devoured you, and I turned you to ashes upon the earth in the sight of all who saw you. All who knew you among the peoples are astonished at you; you have become a horror, and shall be no more forever'* (Ezekiel 28:17–19).

The prophet Isaiah also elaborated upon Satan's fall and subsequent shame:

> *'How you are fallen from heaven, O Lucifer, son of the morning! How you are cut down to the ground, you who weakened the nations.... You shall be brought down to Sheol, to the lowest depths of the Pit. Those who see you will gaze at you, and consider you, saying: "Is this the man who made the earth tremble, who shook kingdoms, who made the world as a wilderness and destroyed its cities, who did not open the house of his prisoners".... You are cast out of your grave like an abominable branch, like the garment of those who are slain, thrust through with a sword, who go down to the stones of the pit, like a corpse trodden underfoot...'*
>
> (Isaiah 14:12–19)

In this passage, Satan makes five vainglorious boasts against the Lord and His Throne. In response, God declares that Satan will first of all be thrown into hell; and secondly, gazed upon (made a spectacle); and thirdly, talked about (mocked and scorned); and fourthly, cast out of his grave like a corpse; and fifthly, be desolate (left all alone).

And His Enemies Will Scatter

Because of the inversion in his nature, Satan cannot tolerate the manifest Presence of God. For Satan, exposure to the Holiness of God represents excruciating pain and incalculable anguish. For this reason, the Evil One flees in terror whenever the Glory of the Lord is revealed.

> *'Then they went into Capernaum, and immediately on the Sabbath He entered the synagogue and taught. And they were astonished at His teaching, for He taught them as one having authority, and not as the scribes. Now there was a man in their synagogue with an unclean*

121

spirit. And he cried out, saying, "Let us alone! What have we to do with You, Jesus of Nazareth? Did you come to destroy us? I know who You are – the Holy One of God!" But Jesus rebuked him, saying, "Be quiet, and come out of him!" And when the unclean spirit had convulsed him and cried out with a loud voice, he came out of him.'   (Mark 1:21–26)

Jesus was God manifest in the flesh – the outshining of the Father's Glory, the exact representation of His nature, the fullness of deity in a human body. It was the unclean spirit's encounter with the Holiness of God in the Person of Jesus that caused it to shriek involuntarily, *'Let us alone!'*

Moreover, the testimony of the unclean spirit reveals the effect of the Presence of God upon the powers of darkness: *'Did You come to destroy us?'* The Greek word *'apollumi'*, translated 'destroy', signifies 'to destroy utterly'. According to Dr W.E. Vine, 'the idea is not extinction but ruin, loss, not of being, but of well-being'. In other words, it is extremely unhealthy for demons to be in the Presence of God!

'Then they came to the other side of the sea, to the country of the Gadarenes. And when He had come out of the boat, immediately there met Him out of the tombs a man with an unclean spirit, who had his dwelling among the tombs; and no one could bind him, not even with chains, because he had often been bound with shackles and chains. And the chains had been pulled apart by him, and the shackles broken in pieces; neither could anyone tame him. And always, night and day, he was in the mountains and in the tombs, crying out and cutting himself with stones. When he saw Jesus from afar, he ran and worshipped Him. And he cried out with a loud voice and said, "What have I to do with You, Jesus, Son of the Most High God? I implore You by God that You do not torment me." For He said to him, "Come out of

*the man, unclean spirit!" Then He asked him, "What
is your name?" And he answered, saying, "My name is
Legion; for we are many." And he begged Him earnestly
that He would not send them out of the country . . . '*

(Mark 5:1–10)

Once again, it is instructive to note the demons' response
to the Presence of Jesus. Firstly, the demoniac *'ran and
worshipped Him.'* Archibald Robertson, commenting on
the words, 'Ran and worshipped Him' in *Word Pictures in
the New Testament*, quotes Swete as follows:

'At first perhaps with hostile intentions. The onrush of
the yelling maniac must have tried the newly recovered
confidence of the Twelve. We can imagine their
surprise when, approaching, he threw himself on his
knees.'

In Volume 1 of *Word Studies in the Greek New Testament*, Kenneth Wuest states:

'The "and" connects the fact of the demoniac's unusual behaviour with his usual habit of attacking
strangers who came near his abode. The fact that he
saw Jesus at a distance would not lead him to worship
Him, but to run to Him, and when he drew closer,
the spiritual power and grace that always pervaded the
personality of the Son of God, quieted his spirit and
caused him to fall on his knees in reverence.'

The Greek word *'proskuneo'*, translated 'worshipped', is
'to make obeisance or do reverence to, often by kneeling or
prostration'. Wuest says that it is 'to kiss the hand to
(towards) one in token of reverence, to fall upon the knees
and touch the ground with the forehead as an expression of
profound reverence (to make a *salam*)'. James Strong, in a
definition particularly suited to demonic spirits, says that it

is 'to kiss, like a dog licking his master's hand, to fawn or crouch to'.

Professor Wuest further states that

> 'it is used of homage shown to men of superior rank, or of homage shown to God. Here it speaks of homage to God, the act of worship, for the demon recognizes our Lord as the Son of God. Here we have a being, incorrigible in his nature, destined to be damned for all eternity, one of the cohorts of Satan, bending the knee to God the Son. This is that of which Paul was speaking when he referred to the universal adoration of the Lord Jesus, even by beings under the earth (Philippians 2:10). They are even now bending the knee to the Son of God. In the last analysis, it was not the demoniac who was prostrating himself before the Lord Jesus. He was under the control of the demon, and the latter was the source of the homage paid the Son of God.'[1]

Did you hear that? It was not the man, as much as the demon, that was prostrating itself before the Son of God! Hallelujah!

Secondly, and in response to Jesus' order of expulsion, the demon yelled, *'What have I to do with You, Jesus Son of the Most High God? I implore You by God that You do not torment me.'* The Greek word, *'basanizo'*, translated 'torment', means 'to torture', and answers to the modern-day 'third degree'. Just as brilliant sunlight pains sore and infected eyes, so the Glory of the Holy Son of God tortured the mass of filth and perversion that grovelled at His feet.

Thirdly, the demon *'begged Him earnestly that He would not send them out of the country.'* The verb *'parakaleo'* is a very strong word, indicating 'franticness on the part of the demon'.

The Apostle James sheds further light on the reaction of the powers of darkness to the Presence of God, declaring that demons believe in the existence of the one true

God, and tremble (James 2:19). The Greek word *'phrisso'*, translated 'tremble', means 'to bristle, shiver or shudder'. In colloquial terms, it is referred to as the hair standing up on the back of one's neck, or a chill of fear running down one's spine.

Moreover, James exhorts believers to come under God's authority in every area of their lives, and to resist the devil (James 4:7). The word for 'resist' is *'anthistemi'*, from which we derive the term 'antihistamine'. Literally translated, the verb means 'to cause to stand against', and suggests 'vigorous opposition, brave resistance, standing face-to-face against an adversary, and standing one's ground'. This is precisely the stance that Jesus adopted when He encountered the powers of darkness, whether in the wilderness temptation when He said, *'Away with you Satan!'* (Matthew 4:10), or in the temptation to avoid the Cross when He likewise answered, *'Get behind Me Satan!'* (Matthew 16:23), or in His preaching/healing ministry when He *'cast out the spirits with a word'* (Matthew 8:16).

Believers who are clothed with the righteousness of Jesus, filled with the Presence of Jesus, and equipped with the power of Jesus, can resist the devil just as Jesus did when He was on earth. This is the essence of the injunction to *'cast out demons in My Name'* (Mark 16:17). According to the Apostle James, the devil should respond to Jesus' followers in the same way that he responded to the Lord when He was on earth. By fleeing in terror from His Presence!

The Wicked Perish at the Presence of God

'Immanuel' – God with us – is more than a wonderful promise; it is a revelation of God's Divine Nature and Eternal Purpose. It is the character of the Lord to be with His people, in the midst of His people, at the head of His people, all around His people! His Nature is to never leave us or forsake us.

When God commanded Israel to go in and possess the

Promised Land, He declared that His Personal Presence would form the vanguard of their army:

> *'For My Angel will go before you and bring you in to the Amorites and the Hittites and the Perizzites and the Canaanites and the Hivites and the Jebusites; and I will cut them off . . . I will send My fear before you, I will cause confusion among all the people to whom you come, and will make all your enemies turn their backs to you.'*
>
> (Exodus 23:23, 27)

Whenever it was time for Israel to move from one encampment to another, Moses, being mindful of this promise, would cry out: *'Rise up, O LORD! Let Your enemies be scattered, and let those who hate You flee before You'* (Numbers 10:35). Moses recognized that Israel's principal battle was not against flesh and blood, but against the principalities and powers and wicked spirits that energized the Canaanites, Hittites and Amorites. Consequently, Israel's most strategic weapon was the Presence of Almighty God in their midst, represented by the Ark of the Covenant on the shoulders of the priests.

Like King David centuries later, Moses would not engage in a military manoeuvre until he heard the 'sound of marching in the tops of the mulberry trees' – until he had an assurance that the Lord would go before him to strike the camp of the enemy.

King David himself echoed Moses' heartcry in Psalm 68, and reiterated the doctrine of strategic dependence on the Presence of God:

> *'Let God arise, let His enemies be scattered; let those also who hate Him flee before Him. As smoke is driven away, so drive them away; as wax melts before the fire, so let the wicked perish at the Presence of God. But let the righteous be glad; let them rejoice before God; yes, let them rejoice exceedingly.'*
>
> (Psalm 68:1–3)

As has been demonstrated throughout history, and most graphically of all, in the life of Jesus of Nazareth, when God arises, His enemies have no alternative but to scatter. Those who hate Him, whether they be wicked spirits or wicked men, must flee before Him.

The Psalmist employs two metaphors to describe the effect of the Holiness of God on wickedness and corruption: *'As smoke is driven away, so drive them away; as wax melts before the fire, so let the wicked perish at the Presence of God.'* The Presence of God is thus depicted as **Wind** and **Fire**, symbols that are consistent with other biblical revelations of the Holy Spirit, the most notable being the Divine visitation on the Day of Pentecost in which the Spirit came as a *rushing mighty wind*, and rested on the heads of the disciples as *tongues of fire* (Acts 2).

Once again, a study of the Hebrew text yields some remarkable insights to the activity that takes place in the spiritual realm when God shows up. The Hebrew word *'puwts'*, translated 'scatter', literally means 'to dash in pieces', and figuratively 'to disperse'. The picture is of an enemy formation attacking a city and encountering such resistance that it is not only driven back, but its entire communication and command structure is shattered. Thus, the 'scattering' of the enemy bespeaks 'total confusion and disarray'.

To the powers of darkness, the manifestation of the Spirit is, to use a figure of speech, like 'putting the cat among the pigeons.' One can imagine the scene in the spiritual realm when Jesus started to exercise His authority and cast out demons: the evil spirits would most probably have been shrieking in terror, running in all directions at once without any sense of order or purpose, colliding with and cursing one another, much like the Philistines in the battle of Michmash, when *'every man's sword was against his neighbour, and there was very great confusion'* (1 Samuel 14:20), or the people of Ammon and Moab who *'stood up against the inhabitants of Mount Seir to utterly kill and destroy them,'* and then *'helped to destroy one another'* (2 Chronicles 20:23).

The covenantal promise of God to His obedient people is that *'the LORD will cause your enemies who rise against you to be defeated before your face; they will come out against you one way and flee before you seven ways'* (Deuteronomy 28:7). The number **one** is symbolic of unified purpose and coordinated action. Thus, the enemy will come against God's people 'as one man' in classic military fashion, but because of the Lord's resistance, they will be forced to flee in seven directions. 'Seven ways' does not signify seven literal points of the compass, but rather, a complete rout. The enemy will be broken on all sides and dispatched in total disarray. Hallelujah!

Even in matters of eschatology, the Apostle Paul sought to focus the attention of believers on the power of God's Presence, as evidenced by his second letter to the Church at Thessalonica.

> *'... when the Lord Jesus is revealed from heaven with His mighty angels, in flaming fire taking vengeance on those who do not know God, and on those who do not obey the gospel of our Lord Jesus Christ. These shall be punished with everlasting destruction from the presence of the Lord and from the glory of His power, when He comes, in that Day, to be glorified in His saints and to be admired among all those who believe...'*
>
> (2 Thessalonians 1:7–10)

There is a day coming when the Lord Jesus will be revealed from heaven with His mighty angels *in flaming fire*, a metaphor that bespeaks the holiness of God. God's holiness is vital and active, so much so, that it is depicted as a blazing fire which consumes everything in its path (Hebrews 12:29).

Notice that it is with a dazzling display of His holiness that the Lord wreaks vengeance on His enemies. And notice further, that the punishment of the wicked constitutes eternal exclusion from the radiance of the face of the Lord and the glorious majesty of His power.

This Scripture obviously refers to the actual, physical, visible return of the Lord. However, **in principle**, it holds true with regard to any revelation of the Lord Jesus by the Holy Spirit. The manifestation of God's Holy Presence judges and punishes and destroys His spiritual opponents. Let me state once again, **Satan cannot stand before the manifest Presence of a Holy God!**

> '*Let no one deceive you by any means; for that Day will not come unless the falling away comes first, and the man of sin is revealed, the son of perdition, who opposes and exalts himself above all that is called God or that is worshipped, so that he sits as God in the temple of God, showing himself that he is God . . . . And then the lawless one will be revealed, whom the Lord will consume with the breath of His mouth and destroy with the brightness of His coming.*'   (2 Thessalonians 2:3–4, 8)

This Scripture, like the earlier quoted passage from 2 Thessalonians chapter one, refers directly to the final era of human history during which the incarnation and champion of wickedness, antichrist, will be revealed and will oppose and exalt himself above every so-called god or object of worship. The 'spirit of antichrist', however, is already in the world, opposing and exalting itself above the Truth as it is in Jesus (1 John 4:1–6).

But thanks be unto God, *He who is in us* (the Holy Spirit – the Spirit of Truth) *is greater than he who is in the world* (the spirit of antichrist – the spirit of error). And whenever the spirit of antichrist is confronted by the Holy Spirit of Truth, the result is the same: It (the spirit of antichrist) is consumed by the breath of the Lord's mouth and is paralysed or brought to nothing by the brightness of His coming! J.B. Rotherham translates the phrase, 'the brightness of His coming' as 'the forthshining of His Presence'.

When God arises – when the Presence and Power of the

Holy Spirit is revealed – His enemies are consumed, paralyzed, brought to nothing, and utterly vanquished!

Falling Before the Presence of God

The supremacy of God's Presence over the powers of darkness is graphically demonstrated in the story of **Dagon**, the Philistine fish-god, and the Ark of the Covenant.

> *'When the Philistines took the ark of God, they brought it into the house of Dagon and set it by Dagon. And when the people of Ashdod arose early in the morning, there was Dagon, fallen on its face to the earth before the ark of the LORD. So they took Dagon and set it in its place again. And when they arose early the next morning, there was Dagon, fallen on its face to the ground before the ark of the LORD. The head of Dagon and both the palms of its hands were broken off on the threshold; only Dagon's torso was left of it.... And when the men of Ashdod saw how it was, they said, "The ark of the God of Israel must not remain with us, for His hand is harsh toward us and Dagon our god."'* (1 Samuel 5:2–4, 7)

Little did they know, but in capturing the Ark of the Covenant and carrying it into the house of Dagon, the Philistines were introducing the Presence of the Most High God into the very citadel of demonic power in the littoral region of the Promised Land.

Light has no fellowship with darkness, and righteousness has nothing in common with lawlessness, so the act of setting the Ark beside Dagon represented war ... a fight to the finish ... the survival of the strongest.

Dagon was the primary god of the Philistine people, with the torso, arms and head of a man, and the lower body of a fish. He was worshipped as the father of Baal. Thus, he can be readily identified as one of the *'principalities, powers, and rulers of the darkness of this age'* of which Paul speaks in Ephesians 6:12, and with whom the people of God contend.

I am not joking when I say that Dagon was no small fish! He personified a concentration of demonic power that made the Philistines cower in fear. However, he met his match, and then some, in the Ark of the Covenant.

When the people of Ashdod came to the temple the following morning, they found the statue of Dagon lying on the ground, having fallen on its face before the Ark of the Covenant in an unmistakable pose of submission and obeisance. Giving their patron deity the benefit of the doubt, the Philistines picked Dagon up and set it in its place. But alas, when they arose early the next morning, they found Dagon fallen on its face to the ground once more before the Ark of the Lord. And this time, Dagon's head and both the palms of his hands were broken off, leaving only the torso intact.

The 'head' represents **authority** and the 'hand' represents **power**. Thus, the authority and power of the satanic principality called Dagon was utterly broken before the Presence of the Lord God of Israel! The significance of this event was not lost on the spiritually aware Philistines, who said, *'The Ark of the God of Israel must not remain with us, for **His hand is harsh towards us and Dagon our god**.'* For years to come the Philistines would not even step on the threshold where the limbs and head of their god had lain in utter defeat.

The life of the Lord Jesus furnishes numerous examples of the overwhelming power of God's Presence, among the most remarkable of which is His encounter with the detachment of the Roman cohort and the Temple police in the Garden of Gethsemane, which issued in His arrest, mock trial, and crucifixion.

> *'Then Judas, having received a detachment of troops, and officers from the chief priests and Pharisees, came there with lanterns, torches, and weapons. Jesus therefore, knowing all things that would come upon Him, went forward and said to them, "Whom are you seeking?" They answered Him, "Jesus of Nazareth." Jesus*

> *said to them, "I am He." And Judas, who betrayed Him,*
> *also stood with them. Now when He said to them, "I am*
> *He," they drew back and fell to the ground.'*

(John 18:3–6)

In his monumental work, *The Life and Times of Jesus the Messiah*, Alfred Edersheim notes that during the Feast of Passover, the Temple was guarded by an armed Cohort, consisting of from 400 to 600 men, so as to prevent or quell any tumult among the numerous pilgrims.

These hardened, battle-trained soldiers were completely unprepared to cope with the Glory and Majesty of the One whom they had come to arrest. Going forward to meet them, Jesus asked, *'Whom are you seeking?'* To the brief and probably contemptuous, *'Jesus of Nazareth,'* He replied, *'I AM.'* The word 'he' is in italics, indicating that it has been inserted by the translators for the sake of grammatical clarity, and is not part of the original text.

God had previously revealed Himself to Moses as I AM WHO I AM – the Eternal, Self-existent One (Exodus 3:14). Thus, with the pronouncement of the words, *'I AM,'* Jesus declared Himself to be God Incarnate – the fullness of God in bodily form, possessing all the attributes of the Sovereign Lord and Creator of the universe.

It would seem that when Jesus spoke the words, *'I AM,'* the Glory of the Lord which for 33 years had been hidden or at least 'filtered' by the veil of His flesh, was momentarily revealed – with devastating consequences! The Apostle John, an eyewitness of the events in Gethsemane, states that the soldiers *'drew back and fell to the ground.'* This is a unique biblical example of what is popularly called 'being slain in the Spirit.'

The Glory of God is like radiation. In fact, the Bible speaks of *'the brightness of His Glory'* (Hebrews 1:3). The Greek word *'apaugasma'* means 'a shining forth, a radiance, an effulgence, as of a light beaming from a luminous body'. Like powerful waves of radiation, the Glory of God shone forth from Jesus' inner being, overwhelming the soldiers with its intensity. This is perfectly consistent with other Scriptural instances in which the emanating Holiness of God sapped men's strength and energy and caused them to fall down in worshipful submission.

When the Heavenly Being appeared to Daniel by the Tigris river, his vigour was turned to frailty and no strength remained in him, and he fell to the ground as in a deep sleep (Daniel 10:5–9). When the glorified Messiah appeared to John on the Isle of Patmos, the aged apostle fell at His feet as if dead (Revelation 1:12–17). At the revelation of God's Holiness, the twenty-four elders fall down before Him who sits on the Throne and worship Him who lives forever and ever (Revelation 4:8–10).

The Presence of God is indeed, a fire that cannot be quenched, a river that cannot be dammed, and a force that cannot be stopped!

Tremble O earth!

In Psalm 114, the writer records the secret of Israel's exodus from Egypt, crossing of the Red Sea, journey through the wilderness, crossing of the Jordan River, and triumphant entry into Canaan.

> *'When Israel went out of Egypt, the house of Jacob from a people of strange language, Judah became His sanctuary, and Israel His dominion. The sea saw it and fled; Jordan turned back. The mountains skipped like rams, the little hills like lambs. What ails you, O sea, that you fled? O Jordan, that you turned back? O mountains, that you skipped like rams? O little hills, like lambs?'*

The Hebrew word *'qodesh'*, translated 'sanctuary', denotes 'a sacred place or thing; that which is set apart exclusively for the purposes of God'. In like manner, the Hebrew word *'memshalah'*, translated 'dominion', means 'rule', and in this case denotes 'the realm over which God rules', or in other words, 'His Kingdom'.

Through covenantal ceremony, Israel was separated unto God and became His dominion, the one people over whom He bore direct rule on the earth. Once again, we are impressed with the realization that **God can only dwell among those who live under His rule**. It is our submission to the Lordship of Messiah that makes the manifest Presence of God a glorious possibility.

> *'Tremble, O earth, at the presence of the Lord, at the presence of the God of Jacob, Who turned the rock into a pool of water, the flint into a fountain of waters.'*

The secret of Israel's success lay in the fact that they were God's chosen people, and that as a result, His Presence was manifested among them. **It is the Presence of God that makes things happen!**

Natural obstacles, human antagonists, and spiritual enemies alike, tremble at the Presence of the Lord. It is His commanding Presence, more than anything else, that makes a road in the desert, cuts a path through the waters, and causes the mountain to be removed and cast into the sea.

The Secret Place

The Presence of God is like an invisible force-field which the powers of darkness are utterly incapable of penetrating. The Psalmist David understood this fact, and learned to live in the 'Secret Place of the Most High.'

> *'One thing I have desired of the LORD, that will I seek: that I may dwell in the house of the LORD all the days of my life, to behold the beauty of the LORD, and to inquire in His temple. For in the time of trouble He shall hide me in His pavilion; in the secret place of His tabernacle He shall hide me; He shall set me high upon a rock. And now my head shall be lifted up above my enemies all*

around me; therefore I will offer sacrifices of joy in His tabernacle; I will sing, yes, I will sing praises to the LORD.' (Psalm 27:4–6)

'*Sok*', the Hebrew word translated 'pavilion', is a derivative of '*sakak*', a primary root, which means 'to entwine', and by implication, 'to fence in, cover over, hedge about, protect', and 'defend'. The Presence of God in His House is thus depicted as a hiding place, a shelter, a refuge, and an inaccessible and unassailable fortress.

In Psalm 31, David envisions the goodness of God toward those who fear His Name, declaring,

> '*You shall hide them in the secret place of Your presence from the plots of man; You shall keep them secretly in a pavilion from the strife of tongues.*' (Psalm 31:20)

J.B. Rotherham puts it this way: '*Thou wilt conceal them in the secrecy of Thine own presence from the conspiracies of men.*' May God help us locate the secret place of His Presence and abide therein, far from the molestation of sin and the oppression of evil.

References

1. *Word Studies in the Greek New Testament* by Kenneth S. Wuest, Eerdmans Publishing Co., Volume 1, p. 102.

Chapter 10

Cities, Behold Your God!

Isaiah was perhaps the most evangelical of all the Old Testament prophets. The meaning of his name, 'Yahweh is Salvation', accurately reflected both the character of his ministry and the content of his message. As the 'Messianic Prophet', he accurately predicted the birth, life and work, and atoning death of the Lord Jesus. Moreover, as the 'Evangelical Prophet', he envisioned a grace that would bring salvation to people of all nations.

It is significant to note the number of references in the prophecy of Isaiah to 'cities' and 'nations'. In chapter 40, for example, the prophet addresses the 'cities of Judah' with a message of hope and deliverance:

> *'O Zion, you who bring good tidings, get up into the high mountain; O Jerusalem, you who bring good tidings, lift up your voice with strength, lift it up, be not afraid; say to the cities of Judah, "Behold your God!" Behold, the Lord God shall come with a strong hand, and His arm shall rule for Him; behold His reward is with Him, and His work before Him. He will feed His flock like a shepherd; He will gather the lambs with His arm, and carry them in His bosom, and gently lead those who are with young.'* (Isaiah 40:9–11)

'*Say to the cities of Judah,*' or by way of international paraphrase, '*Make a proclamation to the cities of the land in which you live.'* What are we to say? *'Behold your God!'*

The Lord God is the God of cities and nations. He has the world on His heart, and that world is becoming increasingly urbanized. Over one-half of the world's population lives in urban centres. In developed nations, the percentage of urban dwellers is much higher, running as high as 90% in some areas. Sociologists predict that by the year 2010, three out of every four people on earth will live in cities.

The prophetic church is charged with the responsibility of annunciating God's plans and purposes to cities and nations. Those plans and purposes have to do with Divine visitation: *'Behold, the Lord God shall come ... '*

But the prerequisite to annunciating God's plans and purposes is habitual communion with the Lord. It is through the intimacy of prayer and worship that we come to know what is on God's heart, understand His ways and perceive His timing.

God's Plan is to Visit Cities

Jesus demonstrated the Father's plan and purpose by going *'about all the cities and villages, teaching ... preaching ... and healing'* (Matthew 9:36). The impact of His Presence was enormous. Entire cities and regions were moved at His coming.

> *'And when He had come into Jerusalem, all the city was moved, saying, "Who is this?" So the multitudes said, "This is Jesus, the prophet from Nazareth of Galilee."'*
> (Matthew 21:10–11)

The Greek word *'seio'*, translated 'moved', means 'to rock, vibrate, move to and fro in violent concussion, agitate, and cause to tremble'. Figuratively, it means 'to throw into a tremor of fear or concern, to quake and shake'. The English words, 'seismic, seismograph and seismology' are derived from this root.

In Volume 1 of *Word Studies in the New Testament*, Dr Marvin Vincent comments: 'Moved is hardly strong enough. It is shaken as by an earthquake.' In other words, Jerusalem was rocked by a spiritual earthquake when Jesus entered the city!

On several occasions the multitudes followed Jesus on foot from the cities, such was the magnetism of His Presence (Matthew 14:13). When Jesus entered a town, people would start running – not just to be with Him, but to bring sick friends and relatives from the surrounding regions to hear His message and to be healed of their infirmities.

Wherever Jesus went, in the cities, the villages, or the rural districts, He was besieged by the sick. Throngs of needy people filled the streets and marketplaces, begging Him for permission to just touch the **tassels** of His garment – and invariably, as many as touched Him in faith were made well (Mark 6:54–56).

Jesus always functioned within the mainstream of the Father's purpose, and steadfastly refused to be diverted by peripheral issues or opportunities. The Father's plan to visit the cities of Judah was uppermost in Jesus' mind and directed the course of His ministry.

After successful meetings in the lake-side city of Capernaum, in which many were healed of diseases and delivered from demons, Jesus departed and went into a deserted place.

> *'And the crowd sought Him and came to Him, and tried to keep Him from leaving them; but He said to them, "I must preach the Kingdom of God to the other cities also, because for this purpose I have been sent." And He was preaching in the synagogues of Galilee (Judea).'*
>
> (Luke 4:42–44)

Jesus was undoubtedly the centre of attention wherever He went. His Presence changed the spiritual climate of every city He entered. The powers of darkness certainly knew who He was, and trembled.

In the same manner, Jesus commissioned His disciples to go into all the world and preach the Gospel to every creature, beginning with the city of Jerusalem. The extent of the early Church's impact on the city can be seen in the High Priest's accusation that the Apostles had *'filled Jerusalem with their doctrine'* (Acts 5:28).

From Jerusalem believers went forth, preaching the Gospel to the cities of Judea and Samaria, and ultimately to the cities of the world. History attests to the way in which the Gospel gripped entire cities and changed the course of nations.

Like the Lord Himself, the message of Jesus commanded the attention of cities and localities. Such was the magnetism of the Gospel in Pisidian Antioch that almost the whole city came together to hear the Word of God! (Acts 13:44). Antioch, by the way, was no small-time country town. Established by the Seleucids and later utilized by the Romans as a chief centre for the pacification of Southern Galatia, Antioch was a main stop on the great eastern trade route from Ephesus to the Euphrates.

The message of Jesus, like the Lord Himself, brought division to cities and nations. Jesus stated that He had not come to bring peace on the earth, as in compromise and appeasement, but rather division. When Paul and Barnabas went to the synagogue in Iconium, they

> *'. . . so spoke that a great multitude both of the Jews and the Greeks believed. But the unbelieving Jews stirred up the Gentiles and poisoned their minds against the brethren. Therefore they stayed there a long time, speaking boldly in the Lord, who was bearing witness to the word of His grace, granting signs and wonders to be done by their hands. But the multitude of the city was divided: part sided with the Jews, and part with the apostles.'* (Acts 14:1–4)

As I observed in my book, *Preparing the Way of the Lord*, a visitation of God will change us forever, for better or for worse. One cannot experience the manifest Presence of God and remain unmoved, unchallenged, undisturbed, and un-involved. A visitation of God, whether to an individual or a city, summons a decision.

Moreover, the preaching of the Gospel of Jesus effectively 'cleansed the heavens' over certain cities, deposing the ruling powers of darkness and destroying bastions of idolatry.

Obeying the supernatural leading of the Holy Spirit to take the Gospel to the continent of Europe, Paul and his team planted a church in the port city of Philippi, and then travelled 90 miles southwest to Thessalonica. The city of Thessalonica was the capital of the Roman province of Macedonia and was the main stop on the famed Via Egnatia, a major Roman military highway that stretched from the western Balkan coast to present-day Istanbul. Possessing a fine natural harbour, Thessalonica also served as a naval base and an important commercial port.

Once again, the preaching of the Gospel brought division to the estimated 200,000 inhabitants of this cosmopolitan city. For three sabbaths, Paul reasoned with the Jews in the synagogue, explaining and demonstrating that the Messiah had to suffer and rise again from the dead, affirming that *'This Jesus whom I preach to you is the Messiah.'*

> *'And some of them were persuaded; and a great multitude of the devout Greeks, and not a few of the leading women, joined Paul and Silas. But the Jews who were not persuaded, becoming envious, took some of the evil men from the marketplace, and gathering a mob, set all the city in an uproar and attacked the house of Jason, and sought to bring them out to the people. But when they did not find them, they dragged Jason and some brethren to the rulers of the city, crying out, "These who have turned the world upside down have come here too. Jason has harboured them, and these are all acting contrary to the decrees of Caesar, saying there is another king –*

> *Jesus." And they troubled the crowd and the rulers of the
> city when they heard these things.'*   (Acts 17:4–8)

This was not a case of shining a little light in a small
corner! Notice the terminology that Luke employs: *'a great
multitude of the devout Greeks ... not a few of the leading
women ... set all the city in an uproar ... turned the world
upside down ... troubled the crowd and the rulers of the city.'*
However, amidst the tumult, the Gospel achieved great
penetration. Describing the effectiveness of his visit to
Thessalonica, Paul wrote:

> *'For our Gospel did not come to you in word only, but
> also in power, and in the Holy Spirit and in much assur-
> ance ... For from you the Word of the Lord has sounded
> forth, not only in Macedonia and Achaia, but also in
> every place. Your faith toward God has gone out ... For
> they themselves declare concerning us what manner of
> entry we had to you, and how you turned to God from
> idols to serve the living and true God, and to wait for His
> Son from heaven, whom He raised from the dead, even
> Jesus who delivers us from the wrath to come.'*
>
> (1 Thessalonians 1:5, 8–10)

One can only speculate on the extent to which idolatry
was spurned and the Gospel embraced. However, the
testimony of the unbelieving Jews, even allowing for over-
wrought emotion and exaggeration, would indicate that a
significant portion of the population already had, or poten-
tially would, come under the sway of the Word of God.
The Gospel of Jesus shook the foundation of First-
Century civilization and eventually transformed the social
structure of the Roman Empire. The social ramifications
of **Immanuel** – a visitation of God – are evident in the
correspondence that passed between Pliny, the new gover-
nor of Bithynia in Asia Minor, and the Emperor Trajan, in
the year 112. *The Story of the Church*, a publication of the
Church of Scotland, notes that:

'Though the Apostle Paul, on attempting to evangelize Bithynia, had been forbidden to enter that field (Acts 16:7), the province had not long to wait for the Gospel. Christianity was early introduced there and made rapid progress (1 Peter 1:1). But when, or by whom, we do not know. It is evident, however, that by the end of the first century Christians were to be found in Bithynia in extraordinary numbers. Persons of all ages and ranks had embraced the "perverse superstition." So widely spread indeed was the new religion that the pagan temples were almost deserted, their sacred rites wellnigh suspended; farmers complained that the trade in fodder for sacrificial victims had seriously declined. Having had no previous experience of dealing with the new religion, Pliny wrote to his close friend the Emperor for instructions.'

Indeed, such was the saving power of the Gospel and the sanctifying effect of God's Presence in the province, that an embarrassingly large number of persons were accused by informers of belonging to the **Christiani** sect. Moreover, a great number of people had already been put to death on obstinately refusing to curse Christ and offer incense to the Emperor's statue. Pliny, however, became uneasy and resolved to sift the matter.

'To his astonishment he discovered that their religion did not at all fit in with the kind of secret society which the popular mind credited to the *Christiani*. No revelation of hideous doings was disclosed, even under torture. All they did – so the puzzled Pliny wrote to Trajan – was to assemble together before dawn on a stated day (Sunday), sing hymns to Christus as a god, and then bind themselves by a solemn pledge (*sacramentum* – the pledge of the Lord's Supper). It was not an oath taken in view of any criminal purpose; it was a pledge never to commit theft or robbery, or adultery, or to break their word by fraud or breach of trust.

143

"After this, their custom is to depart; but they meet together late on to take food, ordinary, harmless food" – not any cannibal banquet, such as popular belief alleged.'[1]

Jerusalem and Ephesus

As we have noted, the New Testament abounds with examples of cities and nations being visited by God. Two outstanding cases in point are the cities of **Jerusalem** (Acts 2 to 6) and **Ephesus** (Acts 19): one, the centre of Jewish spiritual, cultural and political life, and the other, the chief city of provincial Asia, a centre of international trade and the headquarters of a false religious cult – the temple of Artemis, the goddess of love and fertility.

Although the cities of Jerusalem and Ephesus represent totally different sociological environments, the characteristics of Divine visitation in each case are remarkably similar. Indeed, the Gospel of Jesus is the same the world over, producing the same effect and obtaining the same results irrespective of culture, religion or politics.

Divine visitation begins with **the preaching of Jesus the Messiah** – the proclamation of His Lordship; that He is the Sovereign King, the Anointed of God, the Saviour and Judge of the world, the fullness of God, and the Beginning and the End of His eternal purpose.

The apostolic preaching of Messiah brings conviction of sin, and inspires repentance from dead works and obedience to the Truth, which is the essential dynamic of **water baptism** – a return to the ways of God and a complete identification of one's self with the Lord Jesus Messiah.

The move of God is sustained by **the systematic preaching and teaching of the Word**, thus preventing the harvest from being lost. The consistent ministry of God's Word fosters fellowship and worship in the Church and facilitates the disciple-making process (Acts 2:42). It also lays the necessary foundation and establishes the essential structure for an enlarged move of God's Spirit.

God confirms the faithful, systematic preaching of His Word with **signs and wonders** – a new release of His miraculous power and further manifestations of the Spirit. The work of God grows thereby and becomes known to all who live in the city and the surrounding regions.

Through the combined effect of the Word and the Spirit, the Church **impacts the city with the sense of God's Presence**, the reality of Messiah's Lordship, and the awareness of God's Holiness. The Fear of the Lord descends like a blanket on the city's environs and inhabitants; the conviction of the Holy Spirit fills the air; and the Glory of God is seen in the streets. The revelation of God in the city produces reverence in its citizens.

This invariably leads to a mass 'exodus from Egypt' – **the salvation of those who are appointed to Eternal Life** through faith in the atoning death, burial and resurrection of the Lord Jesus. A great multitude leaves the realm of darkness and enters the Kingdom of God's Son.

And in the final analysis, **the Word of the Lord prevails in the city** – principalities and powers are bound and cast down; their hold over people's minds and bodies is broken and their influence in the region is nullified. The city is released to fulfil its destiny in the purpose of God. Social justice is restored and joy abounds. The Kingdom (reign) of God comes and the Will of God is done on earth as it is in Heaven!

Is the above-quoted scenario just a pipe dream, or is it an attainable goal? Furthermore, are there any instances in church history of Divine city-wide visitations which could serve as faith-precedents for modern-day believers?

The New England Revival of 1735

Jonathan Edwards pastored the Congregational Church in Northampton, Massachusetts, a town of approximately two hundred families, from 1724 to 1750. When Edwards took over the leadership of the church from his grandfather, Solomon Stoddard, he found the people 'very insensible of the things of religion'. The congregations of Edwards' day were full of morally respectable rather than spiritually reborn people, who attended church for the social or political benefits which membership conferred.

'It seemed,' Edwards wrote, 'to be a time of extra-ordinary dullness in religion; licentiousness prevailed among the youth of the town; they were many of them very much addicted to night walking, and frequenting the tavern, and lewd practices . . . ' Yet the decadence of North-ampton was relatively mild compared with the rest of the county. The state of society and morals were becoming more and more corrupt, and for a time it appeared as if God had forsaken New England.[2]

Some people, however, began to cry out for revival, and in 1733 Edwards began to see a change. The next year he preached a series of sermons on justification by faith, and when two young people died unexpectedly, his sermons began to penetrate the hardened hearts of his listeners. Toward the end of December 1734,

'the Spirit of God began extraordinarily to set in, and wonderfully to work among us; and there were, very suddenly, one after another, five or six persons, who were, to all appearance, savingly converted, and some of them wrought upon in a very remarkable manner.

Presently upon this a great and earnest concern about the great things of religion and the eternal world became universal in all parts of the town, and among persons of all degrees and all ages; the noise among the dry bones waxed louder and louder; all other talk but about spiritual and eternal things was soon thrown by; all the conversation in all companies, and upon all occasions, was upon these things only, unless so much as was necessary for people carrying on their ordinary secular business. Other discourse than of the things of religion would scarcely be tolerated in any company. The minds of people were wonderfully taken off from the world; it was treated among us as a thing of very little consequence; they seemed to follow their worldly business more as a part of their duty than from any disposition they had to it; the temptation now seemed to lie on the other hand to neglect worldly affairs too much, and to spend too much time in the immediate exercises of religion . . . .

But though the people did not ordinarily neglect their worldly business, yet there then was the reverse of what commonly is: religion was with all classes the great concern, and the world was a thing only by the by. The only thing in their view was to get to the kingdom of heaven, and everyone appeared pressing into it: the engagedness of their hearts in this great concern could not be hid; it appeared in their very countenances. It then was a dreadful thing amongst us to lie out of Christ, in danger every day of dropping into hell; and what persons' minds were intent upon was to escape for their lives, and to *fly from the wrath to come.* All would eagerly lay hold of opportunities for their souls; and were wont very often to meet together in private houses for religious purposes: and such meetings, when appointed, were wont greatly to be thronged.

There was scarcely a single person in the town, either old or young, that was left unconcerned about the great things of the eternal world. Those that were wont to be the vainest and loosest, and those that had been most disposed to and speak slightly of vital and experimental religion, were now generally subject to great awakenings. And the work of conversion was carried on in a most astonishing manner, and increased more and more; souls did, as it were, come by flocks to Jesus Christ. From day to day, for many months together, might be seen evident instances of sinners brought *out of darkness into marvellous light,* and delivered *out of a horrible pit, and from the miry clay, and set upon a rock,* with a *new song of praise to God in their mouths.*

This work of God, as it was carried on, and the number of true saints multiplied, soon made a glorious alteration in the town; so that in the spring and summer following, anno 1735, the town seemed to be full of the presence of God: it never was so full of love, nor so full of joy, and yet so full of distress as it was then. There were remarkable tokens of God's presence in almost every house. It was a time of joy in families on account of salvation being brought to them; parents rejoicing over their children as new born, and husbands over their wives, and wives over their husbands . . . .

Strangers were generally surprised to find things so much beyond what they had heard, and were wont to tell others that the state of the town could not be conceived of by those that had not seen it. The notice that was taken of it by the people that came to town on occasion of the court that sat here in the beginning of March, was very observable. And those that came from the neighbourhood to our public lectures were for the most part remarkably affected. Many that came to town on one occasion or other had their consciences smitten and awakened, and went home with wounded hearts, and with impressions that never wore off till they had hopefully a saving issue; and those that before had serious thoughts, had their awakenings and convictions greatly increased. And there were many instances of persons that came from abroad on visits or on business, that had not been long here before, who were, to all appearance, savingly wrought upon, and partook of the shower of divine blessing that God rained down here, and went home rejoicing; till at length the same work began evidently to appear and prevail in several other towns in the county.'[3]

The visitation of God to Northampton is widely regarded as inaugurating the most significant religious movement in eighteenth-century America – **the Great Awakening**. The outpouring of the Holy Spirit spread to neighbouring Connecticut, New York and New Jersey, ultimately affecting over one hundred towns, and most importantly, preparing the way for the English Apostle, George Whitefield, who arrived in New England in September 1740, and set off on a six-week tour which resulted in the most general awakening the American colonies had yet experienced.

In Boston the crowds soon became too large to be accommodated in any of the churches, and Whitefield took to the open air, preaching his farewell sermon to a congregation estimated at 20,000. The revival continued in Boston for approximately eighteen months, during which time churches were packed, and services were regularly held in homes. It was said that even the very face of Boston seemed to be strangely altered.

Whitefield met with similar success in other parts of the country. Describing the evangelist's visit to Philadelphia, Benjamin Franklin said,

> ' . . . it was wonderful to see the change so soon made in the manners of the inhabitants. From being thoughtless and indifferent about religion, it seemed as if all the world was growing religious; one could not walk through a town in an evening without hearing psalms sung in different families in every street.'[4]

Spiritual revival paved the way for political liberation, and thus contributed indirectly to the American revolution. Most importantly, however, the revival enabled the Spirit of God to acquire a grip on the burgeoning American populace, thus ensuring that the new independent nation would rest on a godly foundation.

From the **Great Awakening** we learn that a city-wide visitation of God can change the course of a nation. Indeed, the pervasion of one town by the Presence of God can initiate national revival!

The Revival in Rome, New York

Charles Grandison Finney, the nineteenth-century American evangelist, preached for over forty years in an atmosphere of continuous revival, during which time more than one million people came to faith in Jesus the Messiah! Wherever Finney went, spiritual life burst into flame, touching whole communities for the Gospel. Biographer Basil Miller said of Finney, '...in an age when there were no amplifiers or mass communications, he spearheaded a revival which literally altered the course of history.'

Finney believed that nothing could be effected in a revival except through prayer and by the Spirit's special aid. In each revival he enlisted united prayer, sometimes with fasting, for the Spirit's engulfment. Finney's special partner-in-prayer, Father Nash, frequently preceded the evangelist, securing a room and giving himself to prayer in preparation for revival. Often Father Nash would not even attend the meetings, choosing instead to lock himself away and pray for the Spirit's outpouring while Finney was preaching.

Typical of the Spirit's effectiveness was the Finney campaign in Rome, New York, during which

> '...deep awe filled the town and the Spirit's convicting power was mightily upon the people. Deluges of Pentecost literally swept through the city, ebbing and flowing in and out of the church into homes, onto the streets, flooding hotels, stores, banks and schools...'[5]

Describing the extraordinary Presence of God in the town, Finney said,

> 'The state of things in the village and in the neighbourhood round about was such that no one could come into the village without feeling awe-stricken with the impression that God was there in a peculiar and wonderful manner. The sheriff of the county resided at

Utica. There were two courthouses in the county, one at Rome and the other at Utica. He afterwards told me that he heard of the state of things at Rome and he together with others had a good deal of laughing in the hotel where he boarded about what they had heard.

One day it was necessary for him to go to Rome. He wanted to see for himself what it was that people talked so much about and what the state of things really was in Rome. He drove on in his one horse sleigh without any particular impression upon his mind at all, until he crossed the old canal, a place about a mile from the town.

Crossing the canal he was suddenly confronted with a divine sense of impending spiritual doom which settled like a pall over his soul and darkened his mind. It was an "awe so deep that he could not shake it off." He felt as if the whole atmosphere was pervaded with God. The nearer he came to the town the heavier seemed the cloud of divine presence.

Coming to the hotel, when the hostler took away his horse, it seemed to the sheriff that the man looked just like he himself felt, "as if he were afraid to speak." They sensed the near presence of God as though they stood at the long-ago Sinai scene and heard the divine Voice and its thunders and rumbling shaking the mountain.

Finding the man with whom he had business, he could not attend to it, for "they all were manifestly so much impressed that they could hardly attend to business." At the table the sheriff had to leave abruptly and go to the window "to divert his attentions and keep from weeping." He observed that everybody else appeared to feel just as he did. Such an awe, such a solemnity, such a state of things, he had never had any conception of before.'[6]

The sheriff didn't attend the meeting, but returned to Utica. However, he never made mockery of the things of

God or laughed at Finney's revivals again. When the campaign moved to Utica shortly afterwards, the sheriff attended one of the services. While Finney preached, the sheriff fell to his knees, and upon returning to his room, made a full commitment to Christ. Soon he led the hotel keeper to the Master.

> 'The Spirit took powerful hold in that house ... Indeed that largest hotel in the town became a centre of spiritual influence and many were converted there. The stages as they passed through stopped at the hotel, and so powerful was the impression in the community that I heard of several cases of persons that just stopped for a meal, or to spend a night, being powerfully convicted and converted before they left the town.
>
> It was the common remark that nobody could be in this place or in Rome during the time or pass through either without "being aware of the presence of God"; that a divine influence seemed to pervade the place and the whole atmosphere to be instinct with a divine life.'[7]

This scenario was more or less repeated throughout the United States and Great Britain as God took hold of towns and cities and manifested His Presence, demonstrated His Power and revealed His Glory through the preaching of His servant and in response to the prayers of His people.

The Azusa Street Revival

Located on a short two-block street in downtown Los Angeles, 321 Azusa is the most famous address in Pentecostal-Charismatic history. In 1906 a Southern Black Holiness preacher by the name of William J. Seymour was invited to preach in a black Nazarene church in Los Angeles. But when Seymour proclaimed that speaking in other tongues was the initial evidence of the Baptism in the Holy Spirit, he was locked out of the Nazarene church. The stranded preacher started holding home prayer meetings, which soon gave way to front-porch street meetings with an audience that numbered in the hundreds. A search of the downtown Los Angeles area turned up an abandoned old building on Azusa Street, variously used as a Methodist Church, a stable and a warehouse. The fledgling band of 'Pentecostals' started holding services there in April of 1906.

The revival continued for three and one-half years at Azusa. Services were held three times a day, seven days a week. God poured out His Spirit mightily, 'as at the beginning.' Sinners were converted, backsliders restored, and proud religionists humbled. People spoke in tongues and prophesied; the sick were miraculously healed until the walls were covered with discarded canes and crutches; people had visions and dreams and revelations of God.

A preacher and a journalist, Frank Bartleman, was personally involved in the Azusa Revival. His book, *How Pentecost came to Los Angeles – How it was in the Beginning*, published in 1925, is a classic Book-of-Acts-style synopsis of the manifestation of the Spirit. He describes, in lucid fashion, the events that precipitated the outpouring of the Spirit in Southern California.

'I went to the Bonnie Brae meeting in the afternoon, and found God working mightily. We had been praying for many months for victory. Jesus was now "showing Himself alive" again to many. The pioneers had broken through, for the multitude to follow. There was a general spirit of humility manifested in the meeting. They were taken up with God. Evidently the Lord had found the little company at last, outside as always, through whom he could have right of way .... A body must be prepared, in repentance and humility, for every outpouring of the Spirit ....

Sunday, April 15, the Lord called me to ten days of special prayer. I felt greatly burdened but had no idea of what He had particularly in mind. But He had a work for me, and wanted to prepare me for it.

Wednesday, April 18, the terrible San Francisco earthquake came, which also devastated the surrounding cities and country. No less than ten thousand lost their lives in San Francisco alone. I felt a deep conviction that the Lord was answering our prayers for a revival in His own way....

The San Francisco earthquake was surely the voice of God to the people on the Pacific Coast. It was used mightily in conviction, for the gracious after revival. In the early "Azusa" days both Heaven and Hell seemed to have come to town. Men were at the breaking point. Conviction was mightily on the people. They would fly to pieces even on the street, almost without provocation. A very "dead line" seemed to be drawn around "Azusa Mission," by the Spirit. When men came within two or three blocks of the place they were seized with conviction....

The work was getting clearer and stronger at "Azusa." God was working mightily.... Divine love was wonderfully manifest in the meetings. They would not even allow an unkind word said against their opposers, or the churches. The message was the love of God. It was a sort of "first love" of the early church returned. The "baptism" as we received it in the beginning did not allow us to think, speak, or hear evil of any man. The Spirit was very sensitive, tender as a dove.... We knew the moment we had grieved the Spirit, by an unkind thought or word. We seemed to live in a sea of pure divine love. The Lord fought our battles for us in those days. We committed ourselves to His judgment fully in all matters, never seeking to even defend the work or ourselves. We lived in His wonderful, immediate Presence. And nothing contrary to His pure Spirit was allowed there....

Brother Seymour generally sat behind two empty shoe boxes, one on top of the other. He usually kept his head inside the top one during the meeting, in prayer. There was no pride there. The services ran almost continuously. Seeking souls could be found under the power almost any hour, night and day. The place was never closed nor empty. The people came to meet God. He was always there. Hence a continuous meeting. The meeting did not depend on the human leader. God's Presence became more and more wonderful. In that old building, with its low rafters and bare floors, God took strong men and women to pieces, and put them together again, for His glory ....

... We were shut up to God in prayer in the meetings, our minds on Him. All obeyed God, in meekness and humility. In honour we "preferred one another." The Lord was liable to burst through any one. We prayed for this continually. Some one would finally get up anointed for the message. All seemed to recognize this and gave way. It might be a child, a woman, or a man. It might be from the back seat, or from the front. It made no difference. We rejoiced that God was working. No one wished to show himself. We thought only of obeying God. In fact there was an atmosphere of God there that forbade any one but a fool attempting to put himself forward without the real anointing. And such did not last long. The meetings were controlled by the Spirit, from the throne. Those were truly wonderful days. I often said that I would rather live six months at that time than fifty years of ordinary life ....

Someone might be speaking. Suddenly the Spirit would fall upon the congregation. God Himself would give the altar call. Men would fall all over the house, like the slain in battle, or rush for the altar en masse, to seek God. The scene often resembled a forest of fallen trees. Such a scene cannot be imitated. I never saw an altar call given in those early days. God Himself would call them. And the preacher knew when to quit. When He spoke we all obeyed. It seemed a fearful thing to hinder or grieve the Spirit. The whole place was steeped in prayer. God was in His holy temple. It was for man to keep silent. The shekinah glory rested there. In fact some claim to have seen the glory by night over the building. I do not doubt it. I have stopped more than once within two blocks of the place and prayed for strength before I dared go on. The Presence of the Lord was so real.'[8]

One of the participants in the Bonnie Brae prayer meeting that birthed the Azusa Street Revival was Sister Emma Cotton. She was present on April 9th, 1906, when the power of God fell upon the praying saints, and seven received the Baptism in the Spirit and began to speak in tongues. The shouts of praise were so tremendous that it was soon noised abroad that there was a gracious visitation from on high. Sister Cotton wrote:

'People came from everywhere. By the next morning there was no getting near the house. As the people came they would fall under the power, and the whole city was stirred. The sick were healed and sinners were saved just as they came in. Then they went out to find another meeting place and they found an old discarded building on Azusa Street that had been used for a Methodist church but had been vacant for years. It seemed to have been waiting for the Lord, and there began the great world-wide revival. People came from all over the country by the hundreds and thousands. That meeting lasted for three years, day and night, without a break.'[9]

A distinguished Pentecostal statesman of later years, A.C. Valdez, recalled visiting the Azusa Street Mission as a child in 1906.

'As we came within a block of a two-story, white-painted wooden building, I felt a "pulling sensation." I couldn't have turned away if I wanted to. Inside, the place looked like a big, plain barn. Most of the seats – rough planks on wooden nail kegs – were taken. There were as many black people as white .... As we moved toward an open spot on a rear bench, I suddenly felt a chill. How could that be? It wasn't cold at all. Then the hair on my arms, legs and head began to stand on end. It felt as if I were surrounded by God. I was trembling. So was mother and everybody else.

On the platform, a black man – mother said it was Pastor W.J. Seymour – sat behind two wooden boxes, one on top of the other. They were his pulpit. Now and then he would raise his head and sit erectly, his large lips moving in silent prayer. He was a plain man with a short beard and a glass eye. He didn't seem like a leader to me, but when I saw what was going on, I knew he didn't have to be. Something unusual was happening. In most churches, kids would be running up and down aisles or twisting and turning in their seats. Here the children, seated between their parents – even babies in mothers' arms – were quiet. But it was not their parents who kept them still. Nobody even whispered. All the adults were praying with eyes closed. I knew the Spirit of God was there.

Suddenly, people rose to their feet. Everywhere hands shot toward heaven. Mine went up, and I hadn't tried to raise them. So did the hands of smaller children and even those of babies in the arms of black mothers. Big, strong men began to cry out loud, then women. I felt like crying, too. I didn't know why. I just felt, "Thank you, God, for letting me be here with You." As I looked out over the congregation, another chill ran down my spine. It was as if ocean waves were moving from one end of the congregation to the other – the most thrilling sight I had ever seen. Wave after wave of the Spirit went through the hall, like a breeze over a corn field. Again the crowd settled back into the seats. And prayers began to buzz through the hall. Then tongues of fire suddenly appeared over the heads of some people, and a black man with a shining face leaped to his feet. Out of his mouth poured words in some language I had never heard before. I began to tremble harder than before. When he finished, another black man rose and told us in English what the other man had said. It was a prayer to Jesus!

Occasionally, as Pastor Seymour prayed, his head would bow so low that it disappeared behind the top wooden box. Just when quiet settled over the hall, a white woman came off the bench like a jack-in-the-box. "Oh, my blessed Jesus," she cried out in excitement, "I can see, I can see." She placed her hands over her eyes. "Oh, Jesus, thank you. Thank you for this miracle." And she plunged out into the aisle and began to dance, her open palms reaching toward heaven. "Thank you, Father. I can see. I can see!" Before the night was over, another blind person could see, the deaf could hear and the crippled could walk. It was so exciting! That was my first night of many in over three years at 321 Azusa Street.

Everything about the Azusa Street Mission fascinated me – especially the prayer or "tarrying room" on the second floor. Usually one hundred or more black, brown, and white people prayerfully waited there for the Holy Spirit to come upon them. Dozens of canes, braces, crutches and blackened smoking pipes leaned against the barnlike walls. Many times waves of glory would come over the tarrying room or meeting room, and people would cry out prayers of thanks or praise as they received the baptism in the Holy Spirit. Meetings used to go past midnight and into the early hours of the morning. Hours there seemed like minutes. Sometimes after a wave of glory, a lot of people would speak in tongues. Then a holy quietness would come over the place, followed by a chorus of prayer in languages we had never before heard. Many were slain in the Spirit, buckling to the floor, unconscious, in a beautiful Holy Spirit cloud, and the Lord gave them visions.

How I enjoyed shouting and praising God. During the tarrying we used to break out in songs about Jesus and the Holy Spirit.... Praise about the cleansing and precious blood of Jesus would just spring from our mouths. In between choruses, heavenly music would fill the hall, and we would break into tears. Suddenly the crowd seemed to forget how to sing in English. Out of their mouths would come new languages and lovely harmony that no human beings could have learned. On the ground floor, where services seemed never to end, the metal mailboxes, the Azusa Street Mission's "collection plates," were always filled with coins and paper money. Never did Charles Seymour or any other preacher behind the shoe-box pulpit ask for money. They had faith. All preachers had to do was preach. Anybody who had been blessed by the service gave generously.

Hardly ever did the Azusa Street Mission advertise in newspapers about its services. People heard about them through word of mouth. In the same way that my mother and I felt a strong pull toward the mission, so did others. Many who came said that they knew nothing about Azusa Street and the Holy Spirit meetings until they had visions of the mission and were instructed to go there. Others were moved by an invisible force to attend.... Old-line churches frowned on the Azusa Street Mission's Bible teachings, "so-called miracles," and "noisy meetings." Their members who came just once to Azusa Street services and were found out, were often asked to leave their congregations. Some churches tried hard to get the City of Los Angeles to close down the Azusa Street Mission, but they failed. Individuals, too, worked to break up the meetings.... Not only did people try to break up meetings, they sometimes tried to beat up individuals who left their churches for the Azusa Street Mission.

I was ten when San Francisco was destroyed by earthquake and fire, when the "sound of heaven" was heard in Los Angeles at the Asberry home at 216 Bonnie Brae and then Azusa Street. It was as though some strange, unseen cloud of Holy Ghost conviction had settled down over Los Angeles. Many who were privileged to attend the Azusa meetings had a broken and contrite spirit with unrestrained crying. This was so unusual and unexplainable that few knew exactly what was happening to them and why. The powerful Holy Spirit influence affected people in various strange ways...'[10]

If **Azusa** was a modern upper room, then Los Angeles was a spiritual Jerusalem. Pilgrims came to the **City of Angels** from all over the United States, Canada, and Europe to receive the Baptism in the Holy Spirit, and to return and spread the fire in their own nations, thereby instigating the most significant advance of God's Kingdom since the time of the early church.

The Welsh Revival of 1904

Sensing the danger of the prevailing emphasis upon educational rather than spiritual attainments, and after a 'very heated discussion over the intellectual qualifications for the pulpit', a Welsh evangelist by the name of Seth Joshua 'had it laid upon his heart to pray God to go and take a lad from the coal-mine or from the field, even as He took Elisha from the plough, to revive His work.'

That lad turned out to be Evan Roberts, a former miner and blacksmith, and now, at the age of twenty-six, an accredited candidate for the Calvinistic Methodist ministry of one month's standing. Born in Loughor, Wales, on the Glamorgan and Carmarthenshire border, the main influences upon Roberts' early life were the Bible, Sunday School, and family worship. He possessed a life-long yearning to preach the Gospel, and was seldom seen without his Bible. For ten or eleven years Roberts had prayed for a revival. In his own words, 'I could sit up all night to read or talk about revivals. It was the Spirit that moved me to think about a revival.'

160

In the Spring of 1904, whilst praying by his bedside before retiring, Roberts entered into an experience of such close communion with God that it seemed to remove him out of the body into a third heaven, a personal visitation which continued night after night for about three months. The nearness of God's Presence was such that he could talk of nothing but spiritual things.

The fire of national revival finally fell at a conference at Blaenannerch at the end of September. During the prayer service, Roberts felt a living power pervading his bosom. It took his breath away and caused his legs to tremble exceedingly. The living power became stronger and stronger as each one prayed, until he felt it would tear him apart. He fell on his knees with his arms over the seat in front of him, his face bathed in perspiration and the tears flowing in streams so that he thought it must be blood gushing forth.

'For about two minutes it was terrible. I cried out, "Bend me! Bend me! Bend us! Oh! Oh! Oh! Oh!" As she was wiping my face, Mrs Davies said, "O! amazing grace!" "Yes," I echoed, "O! amazing grace!" It was God's commending His love which bent me, while I saw nothing in it to commend. After I was bent, what a wave of peace flooded my bosom. While I was in this state of jubilation the congregation sang "I am coming, Lord, coming now to Thee." Then the fearful bending of the judgment day came to my mind, and I was filled with compassion for those who must bend at the judgment, and I wept. Following that the salvation of the human soul was solemnly impressed upon me. I felt ablaze with a desire to go through the length and breadth of Wales to tell of the Saviour; and had it been possible, I was willing to pay God for doing so.'[11]

For Evan Roberts, the following days were filled with the compelling need to win the Principality for Christ. The nights were interrupted by visions which spoke of the advance of Christ's kingdom on an unprecedented scale.

On one such night, Roberts' future brother-in-law, Sidney Evans met the young revivalist walking with holy light on his face. 'Evan, what has happened to you?' asked Sidney. 'I had a vision of all Wales being lifted up to heaven. The Holy Spirit is coming – we must get ready. We must have a little band and go all over the country preaching.' He stopped and looked into his friend's face with piercing eyes. 'Do you believe God can give us 100,000 souls now?'

Following some penetrating meetings in Cardiganshire, the Holy Spirit laid Roberts' home town of Loughor on his heart with irresistible compulsion. It was in this embryonic stage of revival that the characteristic emphases of Roberts' future meetings began to emerge: confession, prayer, personal testimony, and above all, obedience to the Holy Spirit.

Within weeks the fire spread to six or seven counties in Wales. The rapidity of the movement was aided by the widespread publicity given to it in the press – both secular and religious. By the end of 1904 some 32,000 converts had been counted, mainly in South Wales, and by the end of 1905 the number of conversions had swelled to 100,000, as envisaged by Evan Roberts.

The churches of Wales were crowded for more than two years. Drunkenness was cut in half and many taverns went bankrupt. It was claimed that 'three months of the revival had done more to sober the country than the temperance effort of many years.' Crime was so diminished that judges were presented with white gloves signifying that there were no cases of murder, assault, rape or robbery or the like to consider. The police became 'unemployed' in many districts.

Bookshops complained of an inadequate supply of Bibles. The coal mines were transformed from arenas of blasphemy into cathedrals of praise. Some colliery managers claimed that the revival had made their workers 'better colliers', while others spoke of 'greater regularity in the attendance of the men at work.' The pit-ponies could no

longer understand the miners' instructions because of the
absence of oaths and curses.

Summarizing the effects of the revival, D.M. Phillips
wrote:

> 'Prayer meetings are held in the trains, and many
> converts are made. The public-houses and beer clubs
> are empty; old debts are paid; jealousy vanishes;
> church and family feuds are healed; great drunkards,
> prize-fighters, and gamblers pray in the services, and
> give their testimony; the chapels throughout the popu-
> lous valleys of Glamorganshire are full every night; all
> denominations have sunk their small differences, and
> co-operate as one body; and the huge processions
> along the streets send a thrill of terror through the
> vilest sinners ... the Revival is the topic in all spheres
> and amongst all sections of society; and strong people
> are overwhelmed by reading the newspaper accounts of
> it.' [12]

Another witness to the revival stated:

> 'Strong men are held in its grip; the Spirit of God stirs
> to their very depths whole neighbourhoods and
> districts. There is a tumult of emotion, an overpower-
> ing influence and a conviction of sin that can only be
> attributed to Divine agency. Personal eloquence,
> magnetism, fervour or mental power do not account
> for it. The only explanation is the one which the
> evangelist gives – "it is all of God." ' [13]

Roberts' own appraisal of the early meetings at Loughor
reads as follows:

> '... the whole place has been stirred, and my heart has
> been set ablaze by the Holy Spirit .... The people hold
> prayer meetings in their homes, family worship is set
> up, and fellowship meetings are held in the steel
> works!' [14]

One particular meeting was

'... characterized by the intensity of conviction felt in it. Scores found themselves on their knees, unable to utter a syllable, and quite overcome with a sense of guilt. Some of these fell in a heap and others cried out pitifully and loudly in their desire for mercy. Meanwhile Evan Roberts was in spiritual agony, the perspiration pouring from his brow, as he prayed that God would glorify His Son and save sinners. So the meeting continued as a mighty spiritual upheaval until the dawn of a new day. People lost all sense of time, and forgot their need for food, and were seemingly kept from physical exhaustion at their daily work.'[15]

The national daily, *The Western Mail*, reported on the 'remarkable religious revival' at Loughor and its effects on the life of the community:

'Shopkeepers are closing earlier in order to get a place in the chapel, and tin and steel workers throng the place in their working clothes. The only theme of conversation among all classes and sects is "Evan Roberts". Even the taprooms of the public-houses are given over to discussion on the origin of the powers possessed by him.'[16]

The revival spawned an extraordinary evangelistic zeal in the hearts of believers, resulting in intense spiritual activity in the local community. Author-historian Eifion Evans notes that

'In many homes in the area there were prayer meetings for most of the day; eternal issues were discussed freely and unashamedly, and, above all a sense of the presence and holiness of God pervaded every area of human experience, at home, at work, in shops and public houses. Eternity seemed inescapably near and real.'[17]

Eifion Evans observed that generally speaking, a common pattern was followed in most areas:

'On hearing of the revival, interdenominational prayer meetings were commenced, with or without preaching services, in which the young people took a prominent part. The effects were usually the same; church members were solemnized and became more fervent in their prayers, numbers were converted, swearing and drunkenness were virtually eliminated, and the over-whelming sense of God's presence made spiritual issues an easy and compelling topic of conversation. An indication of the extent of these influences is the fact that, in the granite quarries of Penmaen-mawr and Llanfairfechan the workmen were holding "prayer meetings of the most impressive character every dinner hour."'[18]

The most outstanding feature of the revival was the extraordinary Presence of God that pervaded Christian meetings, and indeed, entire villages and districts!

William T. Stead, the famous London editor of the *Pall Mall Gazette*, visited the revival and was interviewed on his return by the *London Methodist Times*. Excerpts from the interview reveal glimpses of what it is like to live in the manifest Presence of God, prompting the prophetic question, 'Who can endure the day of His coming and who can stand when He appears?'

' "Well, Mr Stead, you've been to the revival. What do you think of it?"

"Sir," said Mr Stead, "the question is not what I think of it, but what it thinks of me, of you, and all the rest of us. For it is a very real thing, this revival, a live thing which seems to have a power and a grip which may get hold of a good many of us who at present are mere spectators."

"...You speak as if you dreaded the revival coming your way."

"No, that is not so. Dread is not the right word. Awe expresses my sentiment better. For you are in the presence of the unknown ... You have read ghost stories and can imagine what you would feel if you were alone at midnight in the haunted chamber of some old castle and you heard the slow and stealthy step stealing along the corridor where the visitor from another world was said to walk. If you go to South Wales and watch the revival, you will feel pretty much like that. There is something there from the other world. You cannot say whence it came or whither it is going, but it moves and lives and reaches for you all the time. You see men and women go down in sobbing agony before your eyes as the invisible Hand clutches at their heart. And you shudder. It's pretty grim I tell you. If you are afraid of strong emotions, you'd better give the revival a wide berth." '[19]

The Key of Authority

Throughout the Bible, the figure of a 'key' is used to denote **authority**. All authority has been given to the Lord Jesus in heaven and on earth, in both the spiritual and the natural realms (Matthew 28:18). Thus, Messiah Jesus is spoken of as possessing the 'key of David' – the authority to open that which no one else can shut and to shut that which no one else can open (Revelation 3:7).

The exalted Messiah, in turn, delegates His authority – **the keys of the Kingdom of Heaven** – to the Church, giving her the power of attorney to execute His will and accomplish His purpose on the earth. Addressing Peter, as a representative of the Redeemed Community throughout the ages, Jesus said,

> *'... on this rock I will build My church, and the gates of Hades shall not prevail against it. And I will give you the keys of the kingdom of heaven, and whatever you bind on earth will be bound in heaven, and whatever you loose on earth will be loosed in heaven.'* (Matthew 16:18–19)

Jesus also said, In My Name you *'shall cast out demons...'* (Mark 16:17). Baptize disciples *'in the Name of the Father and of the Son and of the Holy Spirit'* (Matthew 28:19). *'Whatever you ask in My Name, that I will do...'* (John 14:13). *'Whatever you ask the Father in My Name He will give you'* (John 16:23).

The secret of the Name of Jesus is the principle of delegated authority! We are born of God's Spirit, imbued with God's nature, called by God's Name, and covenantly bound to Him through the Blood of His Son. We are God's legal representatives on the earth, and as such, are empowered and equipped to speak His Word, perform His works and accomplish His will.

In Old Testament times, the authority of a city was vested in the elders. They would sit in the gate of the city and pass judgment on such matters as murder, rebellion, marital dissension and family strife (Deuteronomy 21, 22 and 25). Moreover, they bore the responsibility of administering the Law of God in the social and domestic affairs of the city (Ruth 4).

In the same manner, the spiritual authority of a city is vested in the elders of the Church, who, through the preaching of God's Word, administer His Law and apply His Kingdom rule to every sphere of personal, family and community life.

Though there be many local congregations, there is only One Church in any given city. The pastors are therefore co-elders of the Lord's people. Together, the pastors and elders constitute the spiritual 'key of authority' in a city. Their effectiveness in spiritual government is not determined by individual talent or performance, but by mutual agreement and co-operation.

167

Individually, we have no hope of ruling over a city in the spiritual realm. But together, as One Body, with every part functioning properly and ministering in its God-appointed sphere, we can demonstrate Messiah's Lordship in all of life.

The 'key of authority' is turned when the pastors and elders come together to humble themselves and pray and seek God's face. The turning of the key then opens the door to a miraculous outpouring of the Spirit upon the city – a visitation from on High!

The Book of Joel affords a pattern of revival and restoration. Interestingly enough, restoration begins with the pastors and elders recognizing the impoverishment of God's people and God's Land.

> *'Hear this, you elders, and give ear, all you inhabitants of the land . . . what the chewing locust left, the swarming locust has eaten; what the swarming locust left, the crawling locust has eaten; what the crawling locust left, the consuming locust has eaten. . . . He has laid waste My vine, and ruined My fig tree; He has stripped it bare and thrown it away; its branches are made white. . . . The field is wasted, the land mourns; for the grain is ruined, the new wine is dried up, the oil fails. . . . Gird yourselves and lament, you priests; wail, you who minister before the altar; come, lie all night in sackcloth, you who minister to my God; for the grain offering and the drink offering are withheld from the house of your God. Consecrate a fast, call a sacred assembly; gather the elders and all the inhabitants of the land into the house of the LORD your God, and cry out to the LORD.'*
>
> (Joel 1:2, 4, 7, 10, 13–14)

Restoration invariably begins with a humbling of ourselves before God – an acknowledgement of need, a confession of sin. If we are really men of God, shepherds of God's flock, we will have the Lord's burden for His people. And the burden of the Lord for restoration will drive us together. The Holy Spirit will apply Divine pressure to our hearts and lives to assemble with our brethren, fellow-elders of the city, in order to humble ourselves before God and seek His face with prayer and fasting.

As the elders begin to pray, a change will take place in the heavens. The powers of darkness which hitherto have operated with little or no restriction because of the divisions in Messiah's Body (see James 3:16) will be bound and cast down by the spiritual authority that is released through the Church's obedience to God.

The anointing that is poured on the 'Head' (eldership) will be transmitted to the whole Body (Psalm 133). Ultimately, every co-operating local church and every participating member in the city will experience a new and increased anointing as a result of the coming together of the pastors and elders.

The Nature and Purpose of Revival

Many talk about revival, but few understand its nature and purpose. Many make reference to the Glory of God, but few understand its manifestation. The danger of tunnel vision, linear thinking, misconception or plain ignorance is that when the long-awaited, much-talked about revival does come, we may fail to recognize it and could even end up persecuting the very thing for which we have prayed.

The pages of the Bible and of church history are littered with the corpses of those who failed to recognize God when He came, and as a result, touched the Glory, resisted the Spirit, and paid the price. Like Jerusalem, they did not know the time of their visitation (Luke 19:41–44).

How can such a calamity be averted? The first step, obviously, is to hunger and thirst after righteousness, which, in practical terms means to seek God for a revelation of His will and purpose. Secondly, to evaluate the whole counsel of God with regard to a particular revelation (Acts 20:27). The Holy Spirit desires to guide us into **all** truth (John 16:13), and we need to have a corresponding love for **all** truth, not just for a particular theme or emphasis.

The prophecy of Isaiah gives a balanced perspective of the nature and purpose of Divine visitation. The Messiah is depicted as coming **with a strong hand** (in great power and authority), **to rule** (as King in the hearts and lives of His people) and **to reward** (as Judge, recompensing both good and evil). Such a ministry is at once awesome and glorious, splendid and severe.

On the other hand, the Lord Jesus is also depicted as the **Good Shepherd** who comes in **gentleness** (love, mercy and grace), to **feed** His flock (nourishing them unto maturity), to **gather** the lambs (placing the solitary in families and building the local church), to **carry** them in His bosom (holding them in the tender embrace of covenant love and sustaining them with the strength of His arm), and to **gently** lead those that are with young (understanding their frailty and patiently leading them to pasture).

Both word pictures represent valid and necessary aspects of a visitation of God. We cannot have one without the other. Messiah comes as King and Shepherd. A true visitation of God expresses the full revelation of His character: absolute holiness and amazing grace; righteous judgment and tender mercy; firm discipline and loving care.

A case in point is the story of Ananias and Sapphira in Acts chapter 5. The grace of God was mightily at work in Jerusalem, saving souls, healing bodies, restoring marriages, driving out demons, and supplying material needs. The theme song of the Church could well have been 'God is so good!'

Yet in the midst of His manifested goodness, the Lord did something terrible. He struck Ananias and Sapphira dead because of their hypocrisy and deceit. How shocking! Was it because the Lord suffered a lapse in concentration, or maybe, just maybe, because righteous judgment constitutes as integral a part of the Divine nature as healing mercy?

Reverential awe came upon all the Church and upon all

who heard about this incident. Here indeed was living proof of the *'goodness and severity of God'* (Romans 11:22), the year of the Lord's favour *'and the day of vengeance of our God'* (Isaiah 61:2). From that point on, the Church walked in *'the fear of the Lord in the comfort of the Holy Spirit'* (Acts 9:31).

What then should we look for in a visitation of God? The sons of Korah give us the answer in their prayer for revival in Psalm 85:

> *'Mercy and truth have met together, righteousness and peace have kissed. Truth shall spring out of the earth, and righteousness shall look down from heaven. Yes, the LORD will give what is good; and our land will yield its increase. Righteousness will go before Him, and shall make His footsteps our pathway.'* (Psalm 85:10–13)

A balanced blend of mercy and truth, righteousness and peace, as seen in the Person of Jesus our Lord!

References

1. *The Story of the Church*, The Church of Scotland Publications Committee, Edinburgh, 1934, Vol. III, p. 87.
2. *Reviving Revivals* by Harold A. Fischer, Gospel Publishing House, p. 153.
3. *A Faithful Narrative of the Surprising Work of God* by Jonathan Edwards, Baker Book House, pp. 15–19.
4. *Reviving Revivals* by Harold A. Fischer, Gospel Publishing House, p. 155.
5. *Charles Finney* by Basil Miller, Bethany House Publishers, p. 116.
6. *Charles Finney* by Basil Miller, Bethany House Publishers, pp. 116–118.
7. *Charles Finney* by Basil Miller, Bethany House Publishers, pp. 118–119.
8. *Azusa Street* by Frank Bartleman, Logos International, pp. 43–60.
9. *With Signs Following* by Stanley Frodsham, Gospel Publishing House, p. 32.
10. *Fire on Azusa Street* by A.C. Valdez Snr, Gift Publications, pp. 3–11, 23.
11. *The Welsh Revival of 1904* by Eifion Evans, Evangelical Press London, p. 70.

12. *Evan Roberts, The Great Welsh Revivalist and His Work* by D.M. Phillips, p. 275.
13. *The Story of the Welsh Revival*, Fleming H. Revell, p. 5.
14. *The Welsh Revival of 1904* by Eifion Evans, Evangelical Press London, p. 93.
15. *The Welsh Revival of 1904* by Eifion Evans, Evangelical Press London, p. 94.
16. *The Welsh Revival of 1904* by Eifion Evans, Evangelical Press London, pp. 94–95.
17. *The Welsh Revival of 1904* by Eifion Evans, Evangelical Press London, p. 95.
18. *The Welsh Revival of 1904* by Eifion Evans, Evangelical Press London, p. 113.
19. *The Great Revival in Wales* by S.B. Shaw, pp. 56, as quoted in *Revival* by Winkie Pratney, Whitaker House, pp. 177–178.

Chapter 11

Sanctifying the Name of the Lord

Hebrew word and thought espouses the concept of *Kiddush Ha-Shem*, the sanctification of the name of God through acts of courage and sacrifice, such as suffering martyrdom for one's faith.

Kiddush Ha-Shem is rooted in the creed of Judaism, the *Shema*, which enjoins believers to *'love the Lord your God with all your heart, with all your soul, and with all your strength,'* and the Ten Commandments, which stipulate, *'You shall have no other gods before Me ... You shall not make for yourself a carved image ... you shall not bow down to them nor serve them.'*

Kiddush Ha-Shem was invoked by Shadrach, Meshach and Abed-Nego when, on pain of death, they refused to fall down and worship the golden image set up by King Nebuchadnezzar in Babylon. In this case, the Name of the Lord was sanctified, not just by the unflinching loyalty which the Hebrew boys displayed in the face of a certain death, but also by the supernatural deliverance which the Lord accomplished on their behalf (Daniel 3).

Kiddush Ha-Shem is also the underlying concept of the prayer that Jesus taught His disciples to pray.

> *'In this manner, therefore, pray: Our Father in heaven, Hallowed be Your name. Your kingdom come. Your will be done on earth as it is in heaven.'*   (Matthew 6:9–10)

'Our Father in heaven.' The Disciples' Prayer is founded on covenant relationship and unconditional love. We love Him **unconditionally** because He first loved us **unconditionally** (1 John 4:19). And unconditional love for the Father issues in a supreme desire to glorify His Name.

The Greek word *'hagiazo'*, translated 'hallow', means 'to make holy, to set apart for Divine use, to make a person or thing the opposite of "koinos", *common or unclean'. Commenting on the phrase, 'Hallowed be Your Name,'* the Expositor's Greek Testament says:

> 'May God the Father-God of Jesus become the one object of worship all the world over ... How blessed if the whole pantheon could be swept away or fall into contempt, and the one worshipful Divinity be, in fact, worshipped ... The One Name in heaven the One Name on earth, and reverenced on earth as in heaven. Universalism is latent in this opening petition. We cannot imagine Jesus as meaning merely that the national God of Israel may be duly honoured within the bounds of His own people.'[1]

The 'Name of the Lord' bespeaks His nature and character, His personal resources, – Who He is and What He has done. In this sense, the Name of the Lord is far above every other name that is named, not only in this age but also in that which is to come (Ephesians 1:21). The glory of God far outshines the glory of man, and indeed, of any other part of creation.

The prayer, *'Hallowed be Your Name,'* expresses the desire that God may take His rightful place as King and Lord in the hearts of people everywhere. It reflects the longing that God may be seen for Who He really is, and worshipped accordingly.

'Our Father'. Christians are concerned about the honour of God. They are deeply grieved when His Name is blasphemed and His character is besmirched. They groan within themselves when His revelation is perverted and His image is defiled. They long for the truth of God to be made known to the sons of men. Their constant prayer is that people may behold the glory of the Lord and taste of His goodness, and thereby enter into a personal relationship with the Most High.

Signs and Wonders

One of the primary ways in which the Name of the Lord is hallowed or sanctified is through supernatural manifestations of the Holy Spirit, known in biblical parlance as 'signs and wonders'.

The experience of the Children of Israel in Egypt is in many respects typical of the experience of the Church in the world. When Moses and Aaron went in and told Pharaoh, *'Thus says the LORD God of Israel: "Let My people go, that they may hold a feast to Me in the wilderness,"* Pharaoh asked mockingly, *"Who is the LORD, that I should obey His voice to let Israel go? I do not know the LORD, nor will I let Israel go"'* (Exodus 5:1–2).

Pharaoh and the people of Egypt displayed a contempt for the Living God, an attitude that is common in the world today, especially in areas where the Church has lost its 'saltiness' and has ceased to be a viable prophetic witness. God's response to Pharaoh, however, was emphatic:

> *'I will harden Pharaoh's heart, and multiply My signs and My wonders in the land of Egypt. But Pharaoh will not heed you, so that I may lay My hand on Egypt and bring My armies and My people, the children of Israel, out of the land of Egypt by great judgments. And the Egyptians shall know that I am the LORD, when I stretch out My hand on Egypt and bring out the children of Israel from among them.'* (Exodus 7:3–5)

Notice that God said, *'The Egyptians shall know that I am the LORD, when I stretch out My hand on Egypt ...'* Signs

175

and wonders – in this case, the ten plagues – brought the people of Egypt face to face with the reality of God in a way that could not be denied or forgotten.

God further revealed the motivation of His heart and the purpose of His dealings with Egypt, as the Children of Israel approached the Red Sea:

> *'... I will harden Pharaoh's heart, so that he will pursue them; and I will gain honour over Pharaoh and over all his army, that the Egyptians may know that I am the* LORD.' (Exodus 14:4)

Once again, it was through a supernatural act – the parting of the Red Sea, the deliverance of the Children of Israel, and the drowning of the Egyptians – that God gained honour over Pharaoh and his army, and revealed His power and majesty in the eyes of the nations.

The impact of God's supernatural acts was still reverberating on the surrounding nations some forty years later! When the Israelite spies came to the city of Jericho and lodged with the harlot Rahab, she confessed: *'I know that the* LORD *has given you the land, that the terror of you has fallen on us, and that all the inhabitants of the land are faint-hearted because of you. For we have heard how the* LORD *dried up the water of the Red Sea for you when you came out of Egypt ... and as soon as we heard these things, our hearts melted; neither did there remain any more courage in anyone because of you, for the* LORD *your God, He is God in heaven above and on earth beneath'* (Joshua 2:9–11).

God's Attention-Getter

The Hebrew word *'owth'*, translated 'sign', denotes a 'signal', both in the literal sense of a 'flag, beacon, standard, monument, or mark', and in the figurative sense of an 'omen, prodigy, miracle, proof, token or warning'.

'Owth' is used 80 times in the Old Testament, and in most cases refers to 'miraculous signs'. The complementary word

'*mopheth*', (wonder), is often used. '*Mopheth*' comes from the primary root '*yaphah*', meaning 'to be bright'. Thus, '*mopheth*' denotes 'conspicuousness, something unique and outstanding, usually with the connotation of supernatural origin, that commands attention and causes the beholder to marvel'.

The supernatural manifestations of the Holy Spirit are designed to capture the attention of men and nations. They are God's signposts, pointing to Jesus and His finished work on the Cross.

Signs and wonders prepare the way for the effective communication of the Gospel by awakening people's interest in things Divine. Signs and wonders apprise the ignorant and remind the apostate of the reality of God. Signs and wonders sensitize people to the Presence of God, thereby engendering conviction of sin and the fear of the Lord.

> '*Then Philip went down to the city of Samaria and preached Christ to them. And the multitudes with one accord heeded the things spoken by Philip, hearing and seeing the miracles which he did. For unclean spirits, crying with a loud voice, came out of many who were possessed; and many who were paralyzed and lame were healed. And there was great joy in that city.*'
>
> (Acts 8:5–8)

Dr Heinz Cassirer's unique translation of the New Testament clarifies the linkage between receptivity to the Gospel and the supernatural works of the Holy Spirit:

> '...each member of the crowd paying the closest attention to what Philip was saying to them, both because of what they heard and because of their witnessing the miracles which he performed.'[2]

Notice that the Samaritans paid close attention to the Gospel **both because of the authority of the Spoken Word and because of the tangible demonstrations of the power of**

God. Signs and wonders open up individual hearts, and in some cases, entire cities and regions to the Word of God!

Acts chapter thirteen furnishes another example of the ground-breaking role of signs and wonders in the international dissemination of the Gospel. Being sent out by the leaders of the congregation at Antioch and more importantly, by the Holy Spirit Himself, Barnabas and Paul embarked on one of the first major missionary journeys to the Gentiles. Their first port of call was Cyprus, beginning in the eastern township of Salamis and ending in Paphos, on the western side of the island.

Cyprus, being a Roman senatorial province, was presided over by a proconsul named Sergius Paulus, whom the Bible describes as an 'intelligent man'. Possessed of a hunger for spiritual truth, Sergius Paulus called for Barnabas and Saul and sought to hear the Word of God. However, Satan also had his emissary in the proconsulate, a Jew by the name of Bar-Jesus or Elymas, whom the Bible calls a 'sorcerer' and a 'false prophet'.

> *'But Elymas the sorcerer withstood them, seeking to turn the proconsul away from the faith. Then Saul, who also is called Paul, filled with the Holy Spirit, looked intently at him and said, "O full of all deceit and all fraud, you son of the devil, you enemy of all righteousness, will you not cease perverting the straight ways of the Lord? And now, indeed, the hand of the Lord is upon you, and you shall be blind, not seeing the sun for a time." And immediately a dark mist fell on him, and he went around seeking someone to lead him by the hand. Then the proconsul believed, when he saw what had been done, being astonished at the teaching of the Lord.'* (Acts 13:8–12)

Notice that the proconsul believed **when he saw what had been done**, that is, when he saw the dramatic demonstration of God's power. The Greek verb *'ekplesso'*, translated 'astonished', is a very strong word, signifying 'to be exceedingly struck in mind, to drive one out of his senses by a sudden shock'. E.J. Goodspeed says that the proconsul was 'thunderstruck at the Lord's teaching.' J.B. Phillips says that he was 'shaken to the core at the Lord's teaching.' Ronald Knox says that he was 'overcome with awe at the Lord's teaching.' It was not eloquence or intellectualism, but rather, the power and authority of the teaching that startled the proconsul.

Here, at the beginning of the Church's missionary enterprise, we have a landmark conversion of a Gentile ruler – a pattern for future generations of cross-cultural evangelists. If it took the powerful proclamation of the Gospel combined with supernatural manifestations of the Holy Spirit to convince heathen rulers then, what makes us think that it will take anything less today?

Signs and wonders help to break up the fallow ground of unbelief and hardness of heart. They are God's answer to a cynical, passionless generation.

> *'And I will harden Pharaoh's heart, and multiply My signs and My wonders in the land of Egypt.'*
>
> (Exodus 7:3)

Where sin abounds, grace abounds much more. In a time of hardheartedness, God will multiply His signs and wonders as a testimony to the inhabitants of the land. It seems that God will go to any lengths to capture people's attention, awaken them to spiritual realities, convict them of sin, and if possible, cause them to turn to Himself. Indeed, when people violate God's law with impunity, it signals that it is time for God to arise and show forth His power in unusual and astonishing ways (Psalm 119:126).

The Divine Seal of Accreditation

Signs and wonders are not only God's attention-getters to prepare people for the preaching of the Word, they also constitute a Seal of Accreditation on the Word itself.

> *'Men of Israel, hear these words: Jesus of Nazareth, a Man attested by God to you by miracles, wonders, and signs which God did through Him in your midst, as you yourselves also know.'* (Acts 2:22)

Jesus Himself was 'pointed out and exhibited', and thus, 'approved and accredited' by God the Father by means of the miracles, wonders and signs which God did through Him. *'As the Father has sent Me, so I send you, and as the Father has accredited Me, so I accredit you.'* That this is to be the norm for Jesus' followers is apparent from His post-resurrection instructions in Mark chapter 16:

> *'And He said to them, "Go into all the world and preach the gospel to every creature. He who believes and is baptized will be saved; but he who does not believe will be condemned. And these signs will follow those who believe..." And they went out and preached every-where, the Lord working with them and confirming the word through the accompanying signs.'* (Mark 16:15–17, 20)

The Greek word *'bebaioo'*, translated 'confirm', means 'to make firm, establish, secure, corroborate, and guarantee'. If we preach a living Lord Jesus, there must be evidences of His Life. If we preach an all-powerful, all-authoritative Jesus, there must be demonstrations of His power and authority.

There is something in the heart of God that delights to bear witness to the good news of His grace with signs and wonders, various miracles, and gifts of the Holy Spirit (Hebrews 2:4; Acts 14:3). Conversely, one can almost sense the disappointment of the Lord Jesus when He came to Nazareth and could not do many mighty works there because of their unbelief (Matthew 13:58).

In the early days of the Pentecostal revival, Spirit-filled believers called themselves 'Full Gospel'. This term offended some denominational churches which did not believe in the restoration of the gifts of the Spirit, because they felt that Pentecostals were claiming superiority over other Christians. Some exclaimed rather indignantly, 'If you call yourselves Full Gospel, then what are we, Half-Gospel?'

However, theological arguments and denominational bias aside, an objective search of the Scriptures concludes that a 'Full Presentation of the Gospel' or a 'Presentation of the Full Gospel' must include supernatural manifestations of the Holy Spirit.

Consider the testimony of the Apostle Paul in Romans chapter 15:

> *'Therefore I have reason to glory in Christ Jesus in the things which pertain to God. For I will not dare to speak of any of those things which Christ has not accomplished through me, in word and deed, to make the Gentiles obedient – in mighty signs and wonders, by the power of the Spirit of God, so that from Jerusalem and round about to Illyricum I have fully preached the gospel of Christ.'*   (Romans 15:17–20)

Here Paul is testifying of the things which Christ accomplished through him in **word and deed**. He defines the 'deeds' which complemented his 'words', so as to make the Gentiles obedient to the faith – *'mighty signs and wonders by the power of the Spirit of God!'* According to the Apostle Paul, this combination of 'word and deed', 'message and sign', 'teaching and demonstration', constitutes a 'full declaration' or 'complete presentation' of the Gospel of Christ.

Likewise, in 1 Thessalonians 1:5, Paul states: *'For our gospel did not come to you in word only, but also in power, and in the Holy Spirit, and in much assurance . . .'* And in 1 Corinthians 2:4, he says, *'My speech and my preaching* (about the Cross) *were not with persuasive words of human wisdom, but in demonstration of the Spirit and of power, that your faith should not be in the wisdom of men but in the power of God.'*

Regretfully, much of our Gospel presentation has been 'in word only', minus the supernatural manifestations of the Holy Spirit which are so crucial to the Gospel's success. But thank God, this is beginning to change as a new wave of the Holy Spirit encircles the globe.

The Purpose of Signs and Wonders

The prophecy of Ezekiel offers a panoramic overview of God's dealings with Israel and the nations. Israel (Judah), the covenant nation, spurns the Lord, her Redeemer-Husband, and commits spiritual adultery with demons and evil spirits. Sliding from idolatry into apostasy, she contemptuously ignores God's pleadings and warnings. Thus, God has no option but to execute judgment upon her at the hands of the surrounding nations, and in particular, the emerging superpower of Babylon. Thereafter follows a litany of woes – economic and socio-political harassment, armed incursion, military conquest, and finally exile.

However, in the midst of wrath, God remembers mercy. True to the Covenant and to the revelation of His Nature, God promises to regather a remnant to the Land, give them a heart of reverence and obedience, pour out His Spirit upon them, and reveal His Glory in their midst. Moreover, God pledges to judge the nations that seek to destroy His people.

In all of His dealings with Israel, God's primary motivation is the glory of His Holy Name.

> *'I had concern for My holy name, which the house of Israel had profaned among the nations wherever they went. Therefore say to the house of Israel, "Thus says the Lord GOD: 'I do not do this for your sake, O house of Israel, but for My holy name's sake, which you have profaned among the nations wherever you went. And I will sanctify My great name, which has been profaned*

among the nations, which you have profaned in their midst; and the nations shall know that I am the LORD,' says the Lord GOD, 'when I am hallowed in you before their eyes.' " '   (Ezekiel 36:21–23)

The Hebrew word *'chamal'*, translated 'concern', connotes in this and other contexts, 'a very emotional response resulting in decisive action'. For example, the word is used in Proverbs 6:34 of a jealous husband not 'sparing' as he executes vengeance on the man who compromised his wife. In Exodus 2:6 the word is used of Pharaoh's daughter having 'compassion' on the weeping baby Moses after discovering him in the ark. In Malachi 3:17 the word is used of paternal love, declaring that God will 'spare' those who fear Him and who meditate on His Name, just as a man 'spares' his own son who serves him.

Thus, the phrase *'I had concern for My Holy Name'* bespeaks a deep emotional commitment on the part of the Lord to the maintenance of due honour.

Motivation for Signs and Wonders

The Lord said to me on one occasion, 'If you can come to the point where your whole motivation is for the glory of God, then nothing will be impossible unto you.' Motivation is the 'bottom line' of faith. It's not so much a matter of whether or not you can believe for something; the question is, why do you want it?

The Apostle James points out that impure motivation is one of the chief causes of unanswered prayer (James 4:3). Moreover, the writer of Proverbs warns that although the ways of a man may be pure in his own eyes, the Lord looks beyond the periphery and 'tests the motives' (Proverbs 16:2).

An absence of the miraculous power of God is usually attributed to a lack of faith. However, this is not always the case. Carnal desire and selfish ambition offends God's

Spirit and obstructs God's power just as much as unbelief and disobedience. For this reason, the Apostle Paul urged the Philippians to *'let **nothing** be done through selfish ambition or conceit...'* (Philippians 2:3).

Our primary motivation in believing for a manifestation of the miraculous – signs and wonders – should be the honour of God. It is on this basis, and this basis alone, that God can entrust His power and glory to earthen vessels.

The prophet Elijah is a wonderful case in point. Born and raised in an era of unprecedented idolatry and apostasy, the heart of the young Tishbite was moved to restore honour to the Name of the Lord. After much prayer, and at the bidding of the Spirit of God, the prophet stood in the presence of the decadent king of Israel and proclaimed a drought.

After nearly three years of devastating drought, and with the spectre of famine looming on the horizon, Elijah presented himself to Ahab and delivered this ultimatum: *'Now therefore, send and gather all Israel to me on Mount Carmel, the four hundred and fifty prophets of Baal, and the four hundred prophets of Asherah, who eat at Jezebel's table.'*

When all the people were assembled together, Elijah issued a startling challenge: *'How long will you falter between two opinions? If the LORD is God, follow Him; but if Baal, follow him ... I alone am left a prophet of the LORD; but Baal's prophets are four hundred and fifty men. Therefore let them give us two bulls; and let them choose one bull for themselves, cut it in pieces, and lay it on the wood, but put no fire under it; and I will prepare the other bull, and lay it on the wood, but put no fire under it. Then you call on the name of your gods, and I will call on the name of the LORD; and the God who answers by fire, He is God'* (1 Kings 18:21–24).

After six hours of fruitless crying out, prancing about, and self-mutilation, the prophets of Baal finally gave up. Elijah then called the people to his side and in the sight of the whole assembly repaired the altar of the Lord that was broken down, thus signifying the renewal of Israel's consecration to the Lord.

Having drenched his sacrifice with water in order to emphasize the natural impossibility of the situation, Elijah began to pray. Elijah's prayer reveals the heart of the prophet, and moreover, the kind of motivation that pleases God.

> *'And it came to pass, at the time of the offering of the evening sacrifice, that Elijah the prophet came near and said, "LORD God of Abraham, Isaac, and Israel, let it be known this day that You are God in Israel and I am Your servant, and that I have done all these things at Your word. Hear me, O LORD, hear me, that this people may know that You are the LORD God, and that You have turned their hearts back to You again." Then the fire of the LORD fell and consumed the burnt sacrifice, and the wood and the stones and the dust, and it licked up the water that was in the trench. Now when all the people saw it, they fell on their faces; and they said, "The LORD, He is God! The LORD, He is God!"'*
>
> (1 Kings 18:36–39)

Elijah was consumed with one passion: the honour of God! *'Let it be known this day that You are God in Israel . . . Hear me, O Lord, that this people may know that You are the Lord God, and that You have turned their hearts back to You again.'* More than anything else, Elijah wanted God to regain His rightful place in Israelitish society. And the Lord graced this selfless, God-centred motivation with a rare manifestation of His Presence and an extraordinary demonstration of His power.

Fire is a sign of Divine acceptance and approval, and hence, an attestation to sacrificial purity. The falling of 'holy fire' – the manifestation of God's Presence and the demonstration of His power – is contingent on purity of heart, or in other words, God-centred and God-honouring motives and attitudes.

References

1. *The Expositor's Greek Testament*, Vol. 1, p. 120.
2. *God's New Covenant*, A New Testament Translation by Heinz W. Cassirer, Wm. B. Eerdmans Publishing Co., p. 226.

Chapter 12

I Will Surely Visit You

The Bible pulsates with the promise of Divine visitation. Gazing down the corridor of time with the prophetic eye of faith, the aged patriarch Joseph declared:

> *'I am dying; but God will surely visit you, and bring you out of this land to the land of which He swore to Abraham, to Isaac, and to Jacob.'* (Genesis 50:24)

To emphasize the solemnity of the prophetic promise Joseph took an oath from the children of Israel, declaring once again, *'God will surely visit you,'* and then adding, *'you shall carry up my bones from here.'*

Every generation has the potential of experiencing a visitation of God ... of receiving an outpouring of the Holy Spirit ... of witnessing a revival of holiness and power ... if it meets God's conditions.

The prophet Malachi said, *'The Lord, whom you seek, will suddenly come to His temple'* (Malachi 3:1). Church history affords numerous examples of sudden, sovereign Visitations from on High. As we study the principles and capture the spirit of pioneers who have gone before, hope rises in our hearts for similar and even greater manifestations of God's Glory in our day and generation.

The Holy Spirit at Herrnhut

A new movement of God's Spirit broke forth in Europe in the seventeenth century which subsequently was known as 'Pietism'. The Pietist revival re-emphasized the importance of the New Birth, personal faith and the warmth of Christian experience as a spur to effective mission. It breathed new life into a region exhausted by the Thirty Years' War, and hardened by theological intellectualism and rigid formularization.

One of the central figures of the movement was Philip Jacob Spener, a senior member of the Lutheran clergy in Frankfurt. In his sermons, Spener stressed the value of a life of devotion rather than correct dogma. He began to hold house meetings for prayer, Bible study and the sharing of Christian experience, which quickly multiplied and formed a basis for the Pietist Movement. Pietism restored the vitality of the German Church and bequeathed to the Body of Christ at large a wealth of new hymns and a genuine missionary concern – a spirit of apostleship reminiscent of the first century Church.

Through Spener's godson, Nikolaus Ludwig Count von Zinzendorf, Pietism made its impact on the Moravian community. Zinzendorf's father, a cabinet minister in Saxony, died when he was only six weeks old. The Count was brought up by his grandmother, Baroness von Gersdorf, who was a friend of Spener and a devotee of Pietism. At the age of ten, Zinzendorf was sent to Francke's grammar school at Halle. He and five other Christian boys founded 'The Order of the Grain of Mustard Seed'. They pledged themselves to 'love the whole human family' and to spread the Gospel. During a grand tour of Europe in 1719, Zinzendorf was moved by a painting in the art gallery at Dusseldorf. It was Domenico Feti's *Ecce Homo*, showing Christ wearing the crown of thorns. Its inscription read: 'All this I did for you. What are you doing for me?' There and then Zinzendorf offered himself for Christ's service, instead of service to the state of Saxony.

In 1722 he organized the settlement of a small company of Moravian refugees on his estate at Berthelsdorf. The Moravians were the spiritual descendants of the Czech reformer and martyr, Jan Hus. Driven from their homeland during the Thirty Years' War, they were scattered throughout Europe and lost many members. A few remained, however, and continued to hold services in secret and pray for the rebirth of their church of the United Brethren.

Johann Andreas Rothe, a Pietist, was installed as pastor in the Lutheran church at Berthelsdorf. At his induction the preacher, Melchior Schafer, prophesied that 'God will place a light on these hills which will illumine the whole land.' Zinzendorf's steward suggested a name for this Moravian colony. Since the plot of land lay on the *Hutberg* or Watch Hill, it was called *Herrnhut*, 'The Lord's Watch'. It became a haven for Protestant refugees from all parts of Germany as well as from Moravia and Bohemia. Lutherans, Reformed, Separatists, Anabaptists and Schwenkfelders, as well as United Brethren, were represented in this extraordinary community.

At first it seemed unlikely that people from such an assortment of traditions could cooperate. A malicious fanatic named Kruger threatened to wreck the whole project. 'It looks as if the devil will turn everything upside down,' wrote Schafer in 1727. Yet it was in this very year that the fire of Pentecost was to fall. In May the whole community agreed to accept an apostolic rule drawn up in forty-two statutes. The future of Herrnhut was then decided: It was no longer to be a hive of sectarians but a living congregation of Christ.

At a communion service on August 13th, the Holy Spirit Himself made them one. According to Arvid Gradin, who was present, they 'were so convinced and affected that their hearts were set on fire with new love and faith towards the Saviour, and likewise with burning love towards one another; which moved them so far that of their own accord they embraced one another in tears, and grew together into a holy union among themselves, so raising again as it were out of its ashes that ancient Unity of the Moravian Brethren.'

After this visitation of the Holy Spirit, Zinzendorf became aware that his missionary vision was to be realized through the Moravian Brethren. He emerged as their acknowledged leader and was consecrated as a bishop in 1737. He travelled extensively in Europe, visiting England and also North America. Zinzendorf was a man of many talents – pastor, teacher, theologian, missionary, hymn-writer, liturgist and administrator. His ultimate aim, however, was to unite all Christians in evangelism.

The Moravian renewal birthed what was undoubtedly the most significant missionary movement since the days of the early church. Within thirty years the Moravians had begun missions in at least ten countries. By 1740 they had reached the Virgin Islands, Greenland, Surinam, the Gold Coast, North America and South Africa. Significantly, Moravians and German pietists showed the first real missionary concern for Jews since the early days of the Church.

Their self-sacrifice, love and total commitment to world evangelization are unparalleled in the history of missions. Despite the group's small size, the Moravians sent out hundreds of missionaries in the eighteenth century, and inspired countless others. Wherever the Moravians went with the Gospel, their loving spirit, strong faith and total commitment conveyed the true nature of Christianity so clearly that hundreds of converts were made.

The tiny Moravian community was the acknowledged leader of evangelical missions, both in the number of missionaries in proportion to its membership, and the lengths to which they were prepared to go. In the West Indies Moravian missionaries even sold themselves into slavery in order to preach the Gospel to the inhabitants of the land! One historian has estimated that the Moravian missions achieved more in this period than all the Protestant efforts before them.

There are also clear links between the spiritually vibrant Moravian community and the Evangelical Revival in

England. A London bookseller named James Hutton became the first English member of the Moravian Church, and was to play a leading role in the English Revival. But more importantly, it was a Moravian leader who steered John Wesley towards his dynamic conversion in 1738.

The Wesley brothers first met a group of Moravian missionaries on a voyage to Georgia and were greatly impressed by their spirituality. It was another Moravian, Peter Bohler, who was eventually responsible for counselling John Wesley as he searched for the assurance of saving faith in Christ. And when Wesley wanted to consider the implications of his revolutionary experience, it was to Herrnhut that he went.

Hearts of Fire

There are three important lessons to learn from the Visitation at Herrnhut: firstly, the manifest Presence of God sets people's hearts on fire with love for Messiah and faith in His finished work. Jesus is all and in all. He assumes His rightful place of supremacy in the life of each and everyone who dares to endure the day of His coming and to stand when He appears.

'Did not our heart burn within us while He talked with us on the road, and while He opened the Scriptures to us?' (Luke 24:32).

Fervent Love

Secondly, the manifest Presence of God releases rivers of love in the hearts of Christian believers and thus, promotes unity in the Church. *Agapé* Love is poured out in our hearts in the first instance by the Baptism of the Holy Spirit (Romans 5:5), and is cultivated by successive manifestations of His Presence.

'Since you have purified your souls in obeying the truth through the Spirit in sincere love of the brethren, love one another fervently with a pure heart' (1 Peter 1:22).

Evangelistic Zeal

Thirdly, the manifest Presence of God stimulates the Church to obey Jesus' last command – to go into all the world and preach the Gospel to every creature. It is the Holy Spirit who testifies of Jesus through us (Matthew 10:20). And it is through successive manifestations of the Spirit's Presence that we receive power, in a progressive sense, to be Jesus' witnesses (compare Acts 1:8 with Acts 4:29–31).

'The zeal of the LORD of hosts will perform this' (Isaiah 9:7).

The Herrnhut Visitation with its massive outpouring of Love and worldwide evangelistic implications is strikingly reminiscent of the words of the Lord Jesus in John chapter seventeen – a High Priestly prayer that epitomises His desire for the Church throughout the ages:

> *'That they all may be one, as You, Father, are in Me, and I in You; that they also may be one in Us, that the world may believe that You sent Me. And the glory which You gave Me I have given them, that they may be one just as We are one: I in them, and You in Me; that they may be made perfect in one, and that the world may know that You have sent Me, and have loved them as You have loved Me.'* (John 17:21–23)

'I in them ... that they may be one ... that the world may know.' The Manifest Presence of God ... Christian unity ... and world evangelization.

To which our hearts respond: **'For Yours is the Kingdom, the power and the glory, forever and ever, Amen!'**